Nine to Five and After

Nine to Five
and
After

*The Feminine Art of Living
and Working in the Big City*

by Irene Silverman

Doubleday & Company, Inc.
Garden City, New York
1964

This book is based on a series of six feature
articles which appeared in the New York *Post*.

Library of Congress Catalog Card Number 64-19328
Copyright © 1964 by Irene Silverman
All Rights Reserved
Printed in the United States of America
First Edition

In Memory of My Mother

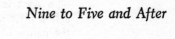

Nine to Five and After

This book is based on
actual interviews, only
the names have been changed.

After College—What? | *chapter I*

"Senior panic," or, will she get a job—What
colleges do and don't do to help—Industrial re-
cruitment on campus: the easy way out—What
makes a girl decide to come to the big city?—
Jobs they want versus jobs they're offered.

In the crowded coffee shop of a New England women's college a group of seniors huddled morosely around a back table.
Above a blaring jukebox and the noisy shouts of underclass-
men hailing each other across the room their conversation—
which was progressing in fits and starts—was barely audible.

". . . have to start applying now or you might as well forget it," concluded a heavy-set girl in a light blue cardigan
sweater. She waved an official-looking letter at nobody in particular. "Proof," she said glumly.

Another girl reached over and took the letter from her.

" 'Dear Miss Hodge," she read aloud, "thank you for your

inquiry of March 1 about future employment in our company. We regret to inform you that our quota of college-graduate trainees for the coming year has already been filled. Sincerely . . .'"

She trailed off. The rest of the table was silent.

For college seniors March is the cruelest month. Christmas vacation is long past. Midterm exams, which occupied the hopeful B.A. to the exclusion of all else, have come and gone. Graduation day, once impatiently awaited, now looms ahead like the gates of hell, and every hour that passes brings the reluctant senior that much nearer to perdition. Suddenly the future is only three months long.

This phenomenon, recurrent yearly on college campuses all across the country, is known to vocational offices and students alike as "senior panic," or the job trauma.

It is a female disease. Women are the chief sufferers.

There are several reasons for this, not the least being that the average girl, when she first entered college, expected to leave through the kitchen rather than the office door. He'd have the job and she the children.[1]

Unfortunately, however, not every girl with a diploma in her hand has a ring on her finger. Sometime around the middle of her last year the unattached senior realizes that, for a while at least, she'll probably stay single. For the first time in her life she is going to be more or less self-supporting.

Only—how?

"I started looking for a job during spring vacation of sen-

[1] Boys, on the other hand, tend to blueprint their futures before they ever apply to college. All their lives people have been saying to them, "And what are you going to be when you grow up?" Rare is the young man who, by senior year, has not chosen a career. In any case Army service usually awaits and the decision need not be immediate.

ior year," recalled a Skidmore '53 graduate. "I was an English major with vague ideas of taking an M.A. and going on to college teaching.

"But all my closest friends were making plans to work in publishing or advertising in New York. They thought I should at least look into it.

"I was very shy then, and hated interviews. The first place I tried gave me a hard time. The man made me think he knew more about me from my college record than I did myself.

"I went back to school and sulked.

"Then someone told me that another place gave a nice interview, and I went over. They seemed interested in what *I* wanted to do. When they offered me a job in textbooks, I decided to take it and not go on for the M.A.

"Everybody at school thought it was just great."

Quiet, a little wary of the "outside world," easily led, this girl never had a chance against the collective pressures brought on her by well-meaning friends to find a job. She might have made a fine teacher. With luck, she may yet. Now thirty-one, not yet married, still at work for the same firm (the only girl in her class who has never changed her job), she speaks hopefully of leaving "sometime soon" to teach—"to do something I've always wanted to do before I'm too afraid to do it."

Sometimes faculty pressure can be just as insistent as undergraduate, with equally deadly results.

Not long ago a talented Wellesley senior, with the advice and hearty consent of her professors, applied for and was granted a Woodrow Wilson fellowship for graduate study. One of the college's top students, a Junior Phi Bete who had majored in government and minored in Russian, she was also one of the biggest "wheels" on a campus famous for hatching scores of fledgling community-chest presidents every June. Her interest in extracurricular activities was if anything even greater than her pride in scholastic achievement.

She had dated little at college, preferring to spend what little free time she had on clubs, student council, and worthy causes. As a freshman she was a leader in an undergraduate movement that raised several thousand dollars for displaced Hungarian refugees.

Outstanding grades had always come easily to this girl. She attended college on a full-tuition scholarship, having graduated from a large public high school first in a class of six hundred. Good grades came so easily, in fact, that by her senior year she took them more or less for granted. An A was an incidental honor compared with what was, for her, the real challenge posed by extracurricular activities.

In November of her senior year the chairman of her department informed her that he was prepared to recommend her for a Wilson. (Wilsons enable the recipient to undertake one year of graduate study with a view toward becoming a teacher.) Pleased and flattered by his encouragement, she applied, and thought no more of it until the following April.

By that time her interest in student council had grown to a point where she was seriously contemplating a career in government. She took a preliminary series of federal civil-service examinations, passing easily, and seriously began to plan a life as an officer in the foreign service.

Then the announcement of Wilson grants came out, and the government career faded. Teachers and students congratulated her on her fellowship. No one asked her whether she really wanted to be a teacher, and soon she stopped asking herself. She applied to Harvard and was accepted at its graduate school of Russian Studies.

The next six months were disastrous.

Twelve undergraduate credits in the Russian language did not, she quickly found, equip her to compete with graduate students who had either majored in the language or came from homes where it was spoken every day. With so much time to make up in Russian, she fell behind almost immediately in her other courses and for the first time in her life found herself unable to keep up in her work. By November she had lost what little feeling she had for the teaching profession. In January she failed most of her exams and left Cambridge.

The experience left her disillusioned and, for a long while, bitter about liberal-arts colleges.

"I shouldn't have gone to graduate school at all," she says now. "When a professor considers you a good student he at once says, 'Well, of course you'll go on to graduate school.' The trouble with a liberal-arts school is that this assumption is automatically made, and the individual may not know herself well enough to do otherwise.

"Some people adjust very well and can cope with something as devastating—for me—as grad school. But it is tough for someone who has had a certain intellectual standing in college, and then goes into a highly disciplined and very unrewarding grad school. The rewards are not immediate in grad school; they don't come till you get the degree."

In short, the rewards of graduate study are purely intellectual. This girl, despite her brilliant academic record, wanted and needed something more. It is hard to say who came off worse: the Skidmore girl who wanted to be a teacher or the Wellesley girl who did not.

Vocational offices exist partly to head off just such calamities as these. Unfortunately many girls, especially in liberal-arts schools, where guidance is most needed, never get anywhere near the V.O. door.

In a recent survey of 88,000 women graduates in the class of '57, more than 41 per cent reported that they got their first jobs through "direct application on my own." Seventeen per cent found jobs through family or friends; 7 per cent were helped by college professors. About 11 per cent used employment agencies.

College women are notoriously independent when it comes to finding jobs. Many of them seem to view their vocational office's listings with actual distaste, as if they suspected the college of some grim plot to auction off its unwary students to the lowest bidder.

Of the 24 per cent who admitted they were "helped by school placement service," most were teachers, mathematicians, and chemists—fields in which demand perpetually outruns supply—or assistant buyers and retail-store trainees. (Large retail department stores underpay and overwork their trainees to a degree ummatched by any other industry. In this instance maybe those suspicious seniors have a case.)

The same survey, oddly, found that young women who while on campus never used the vocational office strongly supported it after graduation.

"Vocational guidance should begin much earlier than the senior year," ran one typical comment, "if not in the freshman year, then certainly by the time a student must choose her major."

Said another: "At our school, vocational guidance was optional, but I think it should have been required."

Still a third plumped for bigger and better V.O. activity. "Representatives from various employment fields should be brought on campus, not only for interviewing purposes, but for educational and informative sessions or lectures as well."

Some of the larger co-ed universities and women's colleges do invite representatives from industry to conduct just such informal lectures and discussions. Once a senior gets to these meetings she often becomes interested enough to make further inquiries; the only problem is getting her there in the first place.

"I thought, heavens, there'll probably be a hundred girls at the lecture and I'd only get lost in the crowd," recalled a U. of Conn. graduate. "Later I found out there were only ten, and they all went for interviews, and the man remembered every one of them."

Some girls scorn campus recruitment. They consider it the easy way out. Getting a job, they seem to think, should be a long and difficult process, fraught with danger at every step, and the harder the ordeal, the more worthwhile the prize. Alas for them, it isn't always so.

"I wrote letters and [sent] résumés to 23 different firms," fumed one university alumna. "During Easter vacation I visited 11 of them for interviews. Six told me to come again after graduation. Finally three offered me jobs, and I took the one that paid the most—84 dollars a week, which I thought was pretty good for a starting salary." (It is.)

"In the meantime my roommate walked two blocks to the vocational office, spent an hour on an interview, and got offered 90 dollars to start." She looked pained. "Anybody could do *that*," she said indignantly.

The girl who has a job by June and the girl who doesn't usually wind up in the same place by July—New York City.

Graduate students may go to Boston, government girls to Washington, and new brides to Army camps, but the college woman in search of a career heads for the big city. (Unless she happens to be a New Yorker to start with, in which case chances are fifty-fifty that she will look for work in San Francisco.)

New York, as far as the prospective graduate is concerned, is simply the Place to Go after College. It has, so she has heard, more jobs, more theaters, more men,[2] more department stores than any other city. It has impersonal neighbors who not only won't notice whether a girl is home by 3 A.M. but probably won't be home themselves. It has dozens of different neighborhoods to explore. It has the most "interesting people" this side of Paris. Best of all, it has—or is about to have—one's college roommate, half of one's sorority, twenty of one's most intimate friends. In short, New York has everything.

The decision to live and work in the city is often never consciously made. Somewhere along the line a girl just picks it up, like the ability to cook. One resident of Newark, New Jersey, a town that is only twenty minutes by subway from New York, found herself hard put to explain to her unhappy parents when and why she had decided to live in the city. Her mother, who really could not understand why the girl should want to live away from home when it was so close to work, pointed out the financial benefits to be gained by staying in Newark and commuting.

"But I never thought of it," said the girl later. "I had made up my mind, and though I never would have moved too far

[2] Not true, unfortunately. New York is actually one of the seven most "feminized" cities in the U.S., with 94.4 men to every 100 women. (In San Francisco, the most "masculine" city, there are 102.3 men per 100 women.)

away from home, I knew I would come to New York after college. New York is the only place to live." Why? "I simply never thought of anything else," she repeated.

Despite the frantic in-college scramble for jobs, most young women do not find work until graduation day is past and they are settled in their new surroundings. Only 18 per cent of graduates surveyed got their jobs either before graduation or in June. Twenty-three per cent found work in July or August; another 7 per cent began work, presumably after taking the summer off, in October or November. (The remaining 52 per cent, mostly teachers, started in September.)

Everybody knows somebody who walked straight out of college into a job paying 125 dollars a week with a month's time off. Everybody knows somebody who never worked a day in her life until the day she started working for Adlai Stevenson (or David Merrick, or Margaret Mead—take your choice). Everybody knows somebody, only nobody knows anybody who is actually in a position to offer such a job.

The combination of salary plus status is the daily double of the working world. Almost no one manages to hit it right off. Like any horse race it takes planning, patience, and a lot of luck. It is wondrous how many college-educated young women are either ignorant of or refuse to believe in this business axiom.

"Time and again," says the head of a leading New York employment agency, "we have had college graduates, girls with no experience and without typing or shorthand, come in and tell us they are 'willing' to take a 115-dollar-a-week job. They seem to expect to jump right over the starting hurdle and straight into a top-money prestige position."

Some people's visions of glory have about as much relation

to reality as would a fallout shelter at Broadway and 42nd Street.

"One girl told us she would 'do anything, just anything, even scrub floors,' to get into TV; then turned us down flat when we suggested a job typing scripts."

(The hunters are sometimes no more self-inflated than the hunted, by the way. The agency man well remembers the time he ran a classified ad for a "secretary to the world's greatest producer" and five Broadway nabobs called to say they weren't looking for secretaries.)

The gulf dividing the jobs girls dream of from the ones they are offered can be appreciably narrowed if the applicant is willing to dispense with half the status-salary combination. Of the two, prestige is much more easily come by than high pay.

"I wanted a job where I'd be in contact every day with lively, amusing, important people—people who get invited to movie premières and art openings, who do something one day and it's in the papers the next. [The speaker is a Vassar '61 graduate.] Also, I wanted a job where I'd make enough money to pay half the rent on an East Side apartment. I figured I'd have to earn a minimum of 95 dollars a week.

"When I told the agency how much I wanted to earn, they only had a few openings at that price. One was a job as secretary to a man who made corrugated boxes. Boxes! When I said no, they offered another as administrative assistant in an insurance company. I turned that down too.

"Then I explained about wanting something swinging, something where I wouldn't be doing the same routine day after day and seeing the same dull people all the time. So then they said they had just the thing: girl Friday at a big charitable foundation. Good hours, fascinating people, big names walking in and out every minute, contacts that could lead heaven knows where. 'Great,' I said, 'what's the salary?'

" 'Sixty-two to start, with a three-dollar raise after the first three months.' "

After trying two other agencies and getting about the same responses, Vassar '61 stopped to take stock.

"It seemed clear that nowhere in New York could I get a job offering both a fairly high salary and an exciting working day," she said. "If such a thing did exist, and I suppose it does, it could only be gotten by promotion from within the company, or after years of experience in a similar job. Nobody comes off the street without any experience into a job like that.

"So I had to decide whether I wanted to spend the next year or two, assuming I get married and quit work, supporting my landlord or working at something I really enjoyed. The way I finally decided it was this: I have no intention of becoming a lifelong career girl. As I said, I hope to marry before too long. 'Who knows,' I figured, 'I might very well meet a guy who'll want to live in California or Hong Kong, or some other place far away from New York. So while I'm here, and have the independence and the opportunity to do what I like, I might as well do it, because I'll probably never get another chance.

" 'If I took a dull job I'd make money, but I wouldn't meet the people I want to meet or see the city the way I want to see it. If I took a low-paying job, on the other hand, I'd have to live somewhere not very glamorous. But it would only be for a few years, and in the meantime I'd be having fun.' "

She now has a job with the U.N. at 76 dollars a week; shares with another U.N. girl an apartment in a nearby middle-income housing project for 51 dollars apiece per month, and sees—and often is introduced to—just about every news maker in town. She may be right about moving far from New York someday too, if a young Danish legation secretary means what he's been saying.

"Glamorous" jobs are more plentiful than you might think, mainly because girls like Vassar '61 can be counted on to meet their Danish attachés within a few years, thus creating a tremendously high turnover. For a college graduate whose finances are reasonably under control, who has only herself to support and who doesn't care if she shops more often at Ohrbach's than Bergdorf's, they are there for the finding.

Finders keepers.

Wanted: Roommates | *chapter II*

Finding an apartment—Roommates versus singles; why some choose to live alone—High living on a low salary—Budgets—Problems facing the newcomer: men, money, morals.

WANTED—Third Girl to Share Apt.,
Mid-Manhattan, 20–26. Box 31X.

June, the month of graduations and weddings, is notable in the real-estate business for the flurry it brings in small apartments.

Very few girls, unless they are born New Yorkers, have apartments waiting for them when they leave college. The lucky ones have friends or relatives with whom they can stay while they look around; others make their temporary headquarters in hotels or women's residence houses.

Anne Gordon, one of the latter, came to New York on a June Sunday armed with a brand-new Cornell B.A., a graduation gift of a hundred dollars from her parents in Gary, Indiana, and an offer from I.B.M. of a research typist's job. One night in a downtown residence house was enough to convince her that she wanted an apartment of her own.

Of the half-dozen ads she answered, three turned out to be for apartments that cost far too much—over 100 dollars a month. Two were located far from subway stations in lonely and, for a single girl, dangerous areas. The last, centrally located and reasonably priced, required a tenant who was willing to assume the combined duties of superintendent and janitor.

Anne quickly discovered what thousands of young career women already know—that, unless her relatives are supporting her or she is earning a minimum of 90 dollars a week, a girl cannot afford to live alone in New York—not, at least, in a neighborhood that can offer her some degree of safety. (Some girls turn elsewhere for support, and usually find it. One girl living alone in a Madison Avenue flat swears that she is the only one in the building being kept by her parents.)

Anne concluded that half an apartment was better than none. Although she had led an independent life in college, living alone for two of her four years, she now decided that a roommate would be less expense and more company than either an apartment of her own or a single room in a women's residence.

Unfortunately, New York apartments do not always lend themselves to the roommate system quite as easily as college dormitories. Anne had a particularly rough time of it. During the next year, she changed apartments three times.

"In the beginning," she said, "I didn't care so much who I lived with, just so I could get settled somewhere. I knew a girl from Cornell who had graduated a year ahead of me. I didn't know her very well, but I had heard she didn't get along with her roommate and they were looking for a third girl to live with them who might patch things up between them. That was me.

"They turned out to be the messiest people I've ever met, and I've never been fussy about a little dirt. One girl had inherited her grandmother's china—thirty place settings. They had so many dishes that they'd never wash the dirty ones till all the clean ones had been used. The rest would sit for days on end in the sink. Then there were mountains of dirty laundry that they'd just let pile up till they ran out of clean clothes. I cleaned the house for a while till I realized I was the only one cleaning. It was ghastly.

"Also, they were the dullest people I've ever known. They came home from their jobs at 5:30, took off most of their clothes, got out beer and sandwiches, and turned on the TV. Then they'd watch till midnight and never even get up to change the channel.

"These two girls both had B.A.s, but they had no interest in anything, as far as I could see, except maybe getting married.

"I don't know why they acted like they did unless it was the freedom that did it. It was the first time in their lives they hadn't been on a directed path, with nothing and no one pushing them to do anything.

"One of them was an art major who had done badly at college because she was uninterested in art. She worked as a secretary in the art department of a magazine. She neither liked it nor disliked it, as far as I could tell. She just wasn't interested. I heard she was a pretty bad secretary, just sat around and read. I'd known her vaguely from our sorority, and she was never like that before."

Not surprisingly, Anne was a failure at "patching things up" between her two roommates.

"It was hard for us to stay out of each other's way, and there began to be continual teaming up. One girl would say unkind things to me about the other and vice versa. They just wanted to be two against one and didn't care which.

"Finally I couldn't stand it any more and we broke up the apartment.

"I got in touch with my Cornell roommate, who had been living at home but was planning to come to the city. By the time she got here, two months after I'd written, she'd picked up two more girls for the apartment. She wrote me and said, 'O.K.?' and since I knew the other two and liked them I said fine. Actually, I thought anything would be better than what I'd had.

"But we had problems right off. First we couldn't agree on where to live. One girl was from Westchester. She said the West Side was all slums, and she wouldn't consider Greenwich Village. The only place she liked was the Upper East Side.

"The second was from Brookline, Mass. She said the same.

"The third—my roommate—didn't care.

"None of us was making more than 80 dollars a week. I said, 'Who needs the East Side?' Then their parents wrote and said they couldn't live in New York unless they lived on the East Side, so that settled it.

"We got an apartment at 69th Street and Second Avenue for 275 dollars a month. Two bedrooms, two baths, a kitchen, and a dining ell. There was a doorman, potted plants in the lobby, and Muzak in the elevator.

"These girls, it seemed, wanted homes just like their parents had. Their attitude was that this was our home, not just a temporary thing, and we should make it a home.

"We'd no sooner moved in than they started pouring money into it. They wanted floor-to-ceiling drapery and wall-to-wall carpets. They borrowed a lot of their parents' furniture. One mother gave us an entire kitchen set. Another gave us enough pots and pans for an army.

"I was miserable, partly because I couldn't afford to contribute and partly because I wouldn't. I was darned if I'd ask my parents to ship a trainload of stuff to me from Gary. Not that the girls seemed to mind—they had enough stuff without me.

"The four of us were in that apartment nine months. Things started going bad soon after we moved in.

"The girl from Westchester and the one from Brookline went out and found jobs right away. They wanted a "future" and a career, which was fine. One went to J. Walter Thompson as a typist. The other got a job in Bloomingdale's executive-training program.

"All of us started making outside friends, and then the trouble started. No one's friends liked anyone else's. The Bloomingdale's girl had a very collegiate bunch of friends. She'd invite them all over at the same time the J. Walter Thompson girl would invite her slick ad men. Chaos! *My* friends were completely out of it.

"It wasn't only that, of course—after a while we worked out a schedule on who could have whom, when. It was really the 'togetherness' that I hated most. These girls couldn't understand it if you wanted to be alone. They wanted to control your every move—to be sure, for example, that you were coming 'home' for dinner.

"Well, I met a man I liked who took me *out* to dinner quite often and brought me back around midnight. This was regarded in the apartment, believe it or not, as antisocial. I wasn't coming home to dinner with the family!

"Maybe it was because these girls came from sheltered sub-urbs and weren't accustomed to 'different' people or mi-nority types that made them want to be together so much. But I like to do things alone, and I wasn't about to be a baby sitter for some kid who couldn't go to the supermarket by herself. Honestly! I had to go along! They never went anywhere alone. One girl left for work fifteen minutes early every day so she could ride the subway with another!

"I didn't read a book for six months. I couldn't do a thing by myself; they resented my wanting to. No books, no pri-vacy. No nothing.

"Then there were the little things, like food. After spend-ing all their parents' money on furnishings, they turned out to be very penny pinching with their own salaries. We had a strict budget. Each one contributed 6 dollars a week for food, and each one was expected to eat exactly one-fourth of the groceries. Snacks weren't included because then you'd be eating more than your share. You had to sneak into the kitchen like a thief if you wanted something to eat between meals.

"Finally I saw I had to get out. I wanted to go to graduate school and I knew I couldn't study in that apartment.

"They took my leaving very personally. It was like a di-vorce."

Ann moved, for the third and last time, to a one-room flat on the West Side. She has lived alone in it for a year.

"I love it. I have friends who visit me, and I visit them, and at last I have something resembling a life."

Girls like Anne Gordon, accustomed to independence and freedom of movement, disliking schedules and togetherness, and perhaps not very easy for others to get along with, are much better off living alone right from the start. They only make things difficult for other people and impossible for themselves by trying to share their apartments and lives.

Most of the young women living in New York, whether alone or with roommates, are out-of-towners. Girls who were born and brought up in the city tend to stay with their parents until they marry, especially if they come from religious families or families in which one or both of the parents was born abroad.

Orthodox Jewish and devout Catholic parents in particular hold that a girl belongs with her family until she has a home of her own—and that means a home with a husband, not a temporary apartment shared with another unmarried girl.

There seems to be little outward resistance among these girls to living at home. On a spiritual level, it is part of their tradition. On a practical level, it saves them money. In private, they do express some inner resentment at being kept home—"like small children," said one girl—after they have passed a certain age. The older the girl, the more likely she is to have this feeling.

"I am quite ambivalent about living at home," confessed the twenty-six-year-old daughter of strict Lutheran parents, both of whom were born and brought up in Germany. "My mother and father are modern people, but they have old-fashioned ideas about unmarried girls who live away from home.

"I sometimes think that if I don't marry soon I will move out anyway. Only I fear loneliness. It's good when you have someone around to talk to—even to fight with.

"Sometimes I am content at home; sometimes, I think, I am miserable. It's because I am not happy being single. That carries over. I'd rather be married, with a husband. I want to select my own furniture and dishes and prepare my own meals.

"My mother wants to see me married too, of course. She has a habit of when she's looking at television, when she sees a little baby she'll say, 'Wouldn't that be a cute grandchild?' Sometimes this amuses me, sometimes not. She has enough sense not to do it when I'm in a low mood.

"One of my friends living at home has parents who shut out the marriage question entirely. They say, 'O.K., dear, stay here as long as you want.' Her mother once told my mother, 'My daughter has time, let her do what she wants.' I don't think it's so good for a girl—she is twenty-seven—to be too content at home like that. There's something wrong if she is. But neither do I think parents should make her life so miserable that she'll want to get out. . . ."

For those girls who do live away from home and family, midtown Manhattan is far and away the favorite area. There are probably more young working women living between 50th and 96th streets than in the four other boroughs combined.

There are certainly more women than men, an unpleasant fact of life that each must learn for herself. Here's where a roommate can be a bonanza. When two share an apartment, the odds on a girl's being asked out for an evening are doubled. He'd be a cad to refuse to bring along a friend for her roommate.

Good roommates are ubiquitous creatures. They have a way of popping up just when you want them, like hot toast. It works like so.

The moment of truth has come. They stand before the door, she with her back to it, he with his hand on the knob. "Aren't you going to ask me in for a drink?" he suggests.

She can't plead a sudden headache; she's been the picture of health all evening. She frowns gently and assumes an expression of despair.

"Oh, Bill, I'd love to [this said in tones of deepest sincerity], but my roommate's asleep and I'd hate to wake her. The walls are so horribly thin."

This works even better when there are three or four living together. One of them is sure to sleep on the couch in the living room, and he certainly can't argue with *that*.

On the other hand, if he's someone special and she has no intention of bidding him good night at the door, friend roommate can always be counted upon to have a date of her own that night. She may spend the evening playing checkers with her cousin on the next block, but she won't be home until at least 2 A.M. Tomorrow, she knows, A will do the same for B.

For a girl who is determined to live high on a low or moderate salary—which means having a good apartment in a good neighborhood, with enough money left after rent is paid to dress nicely, eat well, and still be able to see a few movies and plays—someone to share expenses is almost a necessity. A budget is also, doubtless, a very wise thing to have,[1] and more power to the people who can make one and

[1] According to the Budget Standard Service of the Community Council of Greater New York, a single girl earning 65 dollars a week can estimate cost of living as follows:

Room and Board	$30.00
Lunches at Work	4.50
Clothing	4.20
Personal Grooming	.80
Medical Care	1.65
Cleaning supplies; laundry	2.20
Transportation to Work	1.50
Other transportation	.75
Recreation, Education, Tobacco, and Communication	3.65
Life Insurance	.80
Gifts and Contributions	1.50
Total	$51.55

Taxes amount to about 13 dollars, leaving exactly 45 cents a week to splurge with. Not a very exciting prospect.

stick to it—but half the fun of being a young career woman in New York is lost if a girl has to count pennies at the end of every week.

On the other hand, getting into debt with friends, co-workers, parents, or banks is no picnic for anyone. Luckily, expenses have a way of adjusting themselves. One young gourmet started out saving 20 dollars of her 90-dollar salary each week. She managed it by cutting corners on food, eating inexpensive meals at home every night, and bringing lunches to work.

"Suddenly," she said, "I discovered the variety of restaurants in New York. I haven't been the same since."

Now she spends about 20 dollars a week on food and saves a few dollars here and there when she can. For other girls, other luxuries. The important thing is to be able to indulge, whether it be on food, clothes, vacations, or whatever, without feeling like a criminal or haunting the pawnshops.

The problems of where to live, what to eat, and how much to spend on one or both can be solved at a single stroke by simply taking up residence in a women's hotel. The pros and cons of these hotels, whose charges range all the way from 80 to 220 dollars a month for room and board, have been endlessly debated by generations of young women.

Their detractors say they are nothing but glorified dormitories—all right for perennial freshmen but poison for a self-respecting career girl. Their defenders argue that they eliminate all sorts of bothersome chores such as keeping house, cooking, cleaning, and doing one's own laundry, and thus leave a girl free for more stimulating entertainment. What's more, say the pros, they offer a wide variety of friends to choose from and at the same time provide the privacy and seclusion of single rooms.

It often happens that girls come to New York fully intending to take apartments of their own, stay for what they think will be only a short while at a residence house, grow accustomed to the routine, like it, and decide to remain. Sometimes they like it so much that they become reluctant ever to leave, a situation that the residences themselves consider unhealthy. For this reason most residences limit the length of time a girl can stay. Usually it is a year or two—three at the most.

Residences house as few as sixteen girls and as many as several hundred. Some of the smaller ones can legitimately be charged with collegiateness: in one, "members" vote on the "admission" of each "new girl," who must first dine with them at least twice.

Several residences sponsor mixed theater parties, ski weekends, and bicycle trips. Tiny Henry Hill Pierce House at 209 East 16th Street, sponsored by St. George's Episcopal Church, has bi-monthly dances with the men of a nearby church-supported residence; this accounts for an average of two weddings a year. The YM-YWHA, which maintains a co-ed residence at 92nd Street and Lexington Avenue, averages approximately a marriage a month.

Despite the proximity of so many other young women, residence houses can be just as lonely as one-room apartments. A girl who is shy to begin with will stay shy even though she eats breakfast with eight other girls. One YWCA resident admits that it took two weeks before she ventured to speak to a soul. In the meantime, she recalls, "I went directly to my room, and directly from it outdoors." Shyness and loneliness, according to YWCA officials, are the new arrival's biggest problems.

Probably the city's best-known and most exclusive residence is the Barbizon Hotel for Women at Lexington Avenue and 63rd Street. The Barbizon is run not unlike a tradition-hallowed boarding school. Applications and references from permanent guests are required;[2] first preference on vacant rooms is given to returning "alumnae"; and a social director serves tea every afternoon during the winter months.

All this is not surprising in view of the fact that fully half of the Barbizon's 680 rooms are occupied by eighteen-year-old girls, students at various New York colleges. The Katharine Gibbs Secretarial School alone reserves 200 rooms for its girls and has its own lounge, dining room, supervisor, and nurse.

Hugh Connor, long-time manager of the hotel, says that some people seem to think time and the world stop at the Barbizon. One girl, he swears, married, moved away, got divorced, returned some ten years later, and rushed into the hotel exclaiming, "Oh, hello, Mr. Connor, is Joanie Clark still here?"

The Barbizon's reputation among parents of prospective freshmen can compare favorably with that of any residence in the city. Several parents have gone so far as to defer their daughters' college educations six months or more while waiting for rooms to become available. On one typical morning Hugh Connor's mail brought requests for reservations from Mexico; Deerfield, Massachusetts; Toronto; Nashville, Tennessee; Hamilton, Ohio; Jamaica, West Indies; and Quantico, Virginia.

[2] Not just any references, either. Says the application card: "So that we may maintain a high standard for THE BARBIZON, it is requested that your references be social rather than mercantile or bank references."

If a career girl lives in the city long enough, whether in residence or apartment, sooner or later she comes up against that double-headed monster of the movies: men and morals.

Nobody knows just what percentage of single working girls in New York are virgins, but chances are the statistics are about the same as any place else in the country. New York City is no more "wicked" than any other town. It is just that big-city wickedness seems to get a lot more publicity than small. Somehow people find sin more glamorous when its setting is a Park Avenue penthouse.

Two Syracuse University graduates, both twenty-five, who share an apartment in the east eighties agree that where sex is concerned each girl must decide for herself. One of them is a virgin. The other has had four affairs since graduation in 1959. Interviewed jointly, each said she respected the attitude of the other.

"I can't deny that sex is a problem," said the first girl, "in the sense of should I or should I not. Sometimes, in my lowest moments, I think, 'I'm out of this because everyone else does it.' But that isn't true either.

"Although I don't do it myself, I find it very hard to condemn, provided love is present. I do condemn promiscuity. I know I could never sleep with a man I didn't love. If the man I get engaged to asked me to sleep with him before we were married, I would.

"To me, love is all-important. I get bored just dating. I think when a girl gets to her middle twenties she gets sick of going out, out, out. I'd rather spend a Saturday night at home or with a girl friend than go out with someone who doesn't appeal to me. Even the thought of holding hands with someone I'm not attracted to annoys me.

"What scares me most are the married men. I hope I never fall for a married man."

How much of a girl's actions does she think are determined by the girl, and how much by the man?

"A lot by the man, I think. If somebody really loved you, he wouldn't just want to sleep with you."

Her roommate broke in abruptly. "Nonsense. You can take it for granted that a man wants to sleep with you. It's up to the girl to call the shots. Short of rape, the responsibility is all hers."

"I didn't mean he doesn't *want* to sleep with you," protested the first girl mildly. "I meant if he loved you, there would be other things just as important to him.

"I think," she continued, "that sex is a good yardstick—a good way of finding out if a man really loves you or not. A while ago I was dating a doctor in his early thirties. I really liked him and, from all signs, he really liked me. I honestly thought something would come of it. It wasn't just a physical relationship, I thought.

"Then all of a sudden, after we'd gone out maybe six or eight times, he asked me to go away with him for a weekend. He was very straightforward about it. He said he wanted to have an affair.

"He couldn't understand why I wouldn't. I explained to him—I'm sorry if this sounds corny—that we weren't engaged or anything. He said he didn't want to get married to anybody right now, and he was sorry if he'd given me the wrong impression. Then he left. It really knocked me for a loop."

"That just proves what I was saying," interrupted her roommate.

"No, it doesn't prove anything of the kind. All it proves is that he didn't really love me."

Her roommate looked annoyed. "You worry about love too much," she said. "I'd like to fall in love too, and get married, but that doesn't mean I have to behave like a nun while I'm waiting. In my job [she works for a public-relations firm] I meet many attractive men. I get taken as a matter of course to the kind of parties most girls would give anything to go to—theater premières, art-gallery openings, charity benefits— and after they're over, if I go back with a man to his apartment for a few hours, it's all part of the fun. It doesn't mean I'm going to be any worse a wife when I get married. I'll probably be a much better one, in fact.

"It all has to do with attitude. The things relatives say, for example, just don't bother me any more. I take the advice I care to take, and the rest is for the birds. To my grandparents, a working girl is still a phenomenon. My grandfather says, 'Nice boys won't take you out.' I say, 'Grandpa, I don't like nice boys.'

"I like my life, and I happen to like men too, and I don't see any reason to deny myself something that I like and that isn't hurting anybody." She appealed to her roommate. "Am I hurting you?"

"No."

"We have things worked out," she went on, "so that we stay out of each other's way. When one of us has a man up for dinner the other finds something else to do. We date very different types, so we almost never go out double. Neither of us tries to influence the other. Things work out very well.

"Our only basic difference is over what we've been discussing. As you can imagine, we stay off the topic when we're alone. I never think about it very much at all."

"I do," said the other girl. "I seem to run into it wherever I go. The generalizations people make about single women appall me. So does the curiosity, everybody saying, 'Is she or isn't she? Will she or won't she?'

"But on the whole," she concluded slowly, "you bother yourself about it a whole lot more than other people bother you."

Don't Call Us . . . | *chapter III*

Finding a job—Employment agencies: how they function—Difference in clientele: who goes where and why—Fees charged—"Good" agencies versus "bad"—Employers' opinions.

Finding a job is like finding an apartment. There are various ways to go about it, and if you get the right one in the end it's more a matter of luck than anything else.

One common method of job hunting is through information from friends. News of an opening gets around fast. By the time the boss hears that somebody in his department is getting married and quitting, all of her unemployed friends and relations are lined up for an interview.

The only catch in the grapevine system is that you have to know a fair number of people in business before you can hope to hear of something really good. The grapevine works best for the girls who have been around long enough to skim the gossip on the executive level before it filters through to the typists in the stenographers' pool.

Letters of application often get good results, provided you blanket the field. A girl who can force herself to sit down and type off fifty letters to fifty different companies obviously stands a better chance of getting at least two or three replies than somebody who writes to only a couple of places. (Each letter had better be an original. Carbon copies will hit the secretary's wastebasket faster than she can read "Dear sir.")

Newspaper ads often lead to good jobs, especially if a girl gets up early, or, better yet, retires late. In New York, morning papers go on sale at newsstands around 11 P.M. the previous night. A smart job seeker will pick up an early edition, note the possibilities, and turn up first in line at 9 the next morning when the slowpokes are just plunking down their dimes for the papers. Any morning of the week the dawdlers can be seen sipping coffee or decorating park benches, their white gloves stained gray by newsprint, hopefully reading ads for jobs the early birds have already taken.

If girl and job haven't found each other by high noon at the latest, she might as well spend the rest of the day taking in a good movie. No job—at least no job listed in the want ads—is so hard to fill that not one of the first eight or ten applicants can qualify.

Girls with a B.A. degree should pay particular attention to the listings under "college graduates." That category takes in just about every kind of job available, from

> COLL. GRAD., ENG. MAJOR
> to write book reviews, top publr.

to

> COLL. GRADS, B.S. Home Eco., plan menus.

The competition for these jobs will be tough, but there will be less of it. Thousands of bright young women never attend college; thousands more never graduate.

One good thing about want ads is that they tell where the jobs are, thus saving the applicant the time and trouble of applying to a firm with no openings. What's more, where there is one job advertised there will often be another not mentioned in the paper. Some firms, especially larger ones that have a rapid turnover, like to save money on ad lineage this way. They advertise for one job; then, from the dozens of girls who apply, fill three or four others. The job hunter shouldn't be shy about asking if there's anything else available.

On the debit side newspaper ads can be deceptive. Girls today don't want just any job, and employers know it. They want something that sounds "different," "exciting," "prestigious." The trouble is, *any* job can be made to sound like that.

Say Mr. Jones, a hopeful politician who has an 8×15 office in an inaccessible part of town, needs a secretary. (Mr. Jones often needs a secretary, mainly because they never stay more than six months.)

What he really wants is a girl to answer phones, type letters to prospective constituents, and make readable English out of his tortured politician's prose. But he won't tell *her* that; she'll have to discover it for herself. Here's his approach:

> WRITER, EGGHEAD. . . . Politically
> attuned girl for fast-moving dynamo.
> Some light typing. Downtown.

You can't really blame Mr. Jones. He's only hoping to make a routine job sound so glamorous that the applicants

will come in droves. The more there are of them, the likelier
he is to find one daydreamer who'll believe his ad and not her
eyes.

This kind of advertising sometimes becomes so imaginative
that it ceases to be at all informative. Here's a typical example, culled at random from the Sunday *Times:*

> TV/ART, $85. A happy hunting ground for
> huntress hunting hi and low for heavenly
> haven. Gr. Cent. area.

Maybe they wanted a female hermit to accompany a safari,
but it's doubtful. A routine secretarial job, more likely—or
else they wouldn't have taken so much trouble to disguise
it.

When want ads, friends, relatives, and letters of application
all fail, there remain the employment agencies.

Hundreds of them exist in any big city; in New York there
are more than a thousand. Many can offer jobs running the
gamut from accountant to zoologist, though specialization is
not uncommon. Some cater exclusively to medical personnel;
some to social workers, some to legal stenographers. If you
look hard enough and long enough, you'll even find one or
two that handle nothing but interior decorators.

A few of New York's most reliable agencies specialize in
jobs open only to college graduates. The Alumni Advisory
Association at 541 Madison Avenue is one such.

According to Alice G. King, executive director of this
agency, job seekers get the best results right after Labor Day.
Psychologically, she says, an employer is most willing to hire
in September. He's had his vacation and is back in town
rested and tanned. The heat wave has receded, autumn is on

the way, and all in all it's time he hired himself a new assistant.

Not many college graduates, however, can idle away a whole summer in the vague hope of better prospects in the fall. Most girls want to get to work right away. In June the agencies are jammed.

Fully 75 per cent of the jammers, says Miss King, want "creative" jobs involving "anything to do with publishing or communications," or, if nothing is available in those fields, "anything in the international."

One result of the mass insistence upon creativity is that other fields, even those offering up to twice as much in salaries, are deprived of capable and badly needed talent. The sciences, for example, are wide open for qualified women chemists, biologists, and physicists, but everything seems to work against them. Miss King cites the case of one girl, a trained physicist, who registered with the agency in August. "She was dedicated," she recalls, "not to science but to New York City. She wanted to live right in the heart of town and work as close as possible to 42nd Street and Madison Avenue.

"We had openings for physicists, but nothing in the city. [There are very few opportunities for research in New York itself. Scientific laboratories are clustered, by and large, in neighboring areas: New Jersey, Connecticut, Brooklyn, Long Island and upstate New York.] When she finally found a job—in November—it was as a researcher for a midtown investment-banking firm."

Science suffers the greatest loss of personnel from this kind of thing, but general business, insurance, and service industries are not far behind. For one reason or another—not enough creative opportunity, wrong location, too small a company—college girls miss out on some of the best jobs in town. As one satisfied English major put it, "I'd rather be assistant editor of a steelworkers' house organ than typist in the plushest ad agency in New York."

Not too many young women take this attitude. A college diploma seems to many a passport to the moon. Employment agencies have a far lower percentage of satisfied customers among recent graduates in their first jobs than among older clients with work experience. This is due at least in part to the girls themselves, who, say agency officials, often turn down the first thing that comes along automatically, "thinking it can't be any good," and wind up in an inferior job they hate; or grab the first job they're offered with no intention of keeping it after they hear of a better one.

There are some case-hardened agencies that give special attention to the care and feeding of first-job seekers. Career Blazers, with offices at 5 West 46th Street, is one such. If a job doesn't work out within four months, this agency will find the girl another without charge.

All commercial employment agencies charge standard fees, which are outlined in the application the job hunter receives when she first registers. Fees are governed by state law. In New York, for example, an agency placing a girl in a 60-dollar-a-week permanent job is entitled to charge her up to 91 dollars for the service. If she takes an 80-dollar-a-week job she'll pay the agency up to 173 dollars; for a 100-dollar-a-week job, 260 dollars, and so on.

Some agencies charge a flat rate of one week's salary, no matter how much or how little it may be. These agencies are normally those that cater to clerical workers, bookkeepers, stenographers, and secretaries. The more diversified the job, the more likely it is that the agency will determine its fees like income taxes, on a sliding scale. As salaries go up, so do fees, which are usually figured as a percentage of the first full month's pay. If you make less than 225 dollars a month, for example, you give the agency only 25 per cent of your salary. If you make 400 dollars or more, the agency gets about 60 per cent.

To many out-of-town girls registering for the first time with a New York employment agency, these fees seem exorbitant. One indignant out-of-towner thinks the fault is in the system. "It is outrageous," she says, "that students coming out of school and entering the world for the first time should be faced with such a huge bite out of their first paychecks." On the other hand, it is a fact that commercial agencies, some of which employ dozens of people and have a very high overhead, are entirely dependent upon fees for support. Also, for every girl who makes life easy for an agency there are three who do not.

An agency might carry Miss Black's name on its books for several months, sending her out to dozens of different interviews. When she finally finds employment, however, she'll pay them the same fee as Miss White, who took the first job she was offered the first day she registered. Miss White's fee helps the agency pay for the paper work, records, and files it kept on Miss Black.

Then there's Miss Green, who isn't satisfied with anything she sees and who is determined to work in an air-conditioned, wall-to-wall-carpeted, one-girl-to-every-five-single-men office.

"In general," moaned an agency executive (male), "the girls today are looking for a job on a gold platter. Their only thought is for their own comfort. This applies even to those with no skills, and college girls who can neither type nor take shorthand are particular culprits."

"Sometimes," adds a woman executive at a midtown

agency, "young women refuse to consider jobs not within walking distance of their apartments. Or, when they do accept jobs some way away from their homes, they want to be able to quit at 4:30 so they can beat the subway rush.

"Nothing surprises me any more."

Knowledgeable job hunters are often willing to sacrifice such fringe benefits for jobs that the agencies advertise as "fee pd." Many firms, especially those that do *not* offer air conditioning and all the rest, make it up to their workers by paying their agency fees in whole or in part. This pays off for them, they find, in better employee-employer relations and increased goodwill on both sides. What's more, the boss who picks up the tab runs less risk of being sent unqualified candidates. The agency is usually eager to please the man who pays. There are always exceptions, such as the disenchanted girl who complained that while she was being interviewed for a job her agency called the interviewer to tell him they had four other girls to recommend; then, after the job was finally hers, charged her a flat fee of 400 dollars for the "service."

So it goes. Some agencies are naturally better than others. They charge less, or they have a wider range of jobs listed, or they give more personal consideration to the job seeker. Finding a "good" agency is largely a matter of luck. In the classified pages of the telephone directory they all look alike.

Medium-size firms sometimes maintain their own personnel departments. Large ones almost always do. It's usually the two- or three-man office that must depend upon the agencies for its staff—and here again, this time from an employer's point of view, *caveat emptor* is the watchword.

"My partner and I were straight out of law school when we set up practice seven years ago," recalls a young Midwesterner. "There was barely room enough in the office for a third desk. We needed a legal stenographer-receptionist-telephone answerer-girl Friday; someone who wouldn't care about the clutter but would care about helping make the firm a going business.

"We picked an agency at random from the phone book. The first week they sent us a stream of eighteen-year-olds who hardly stayed in the office long enough to say hello. They'd take one look at the place, say it wasn't quite what they'd had in mind, and leave.

"So we called the agency again, telling them they'd save us a lot of time if they explained the situation in advance to the girls so they wouldn't expect to find all the comforts of a Wall Street law firm. Fine. Then they started sending women who could type but not take dictation, or answer phones in any language but English, or take great shorthand only spell like first graders. When we called to complain the agency told us we were unusually hard to please and we shouldn't expect to find a good legal secretary under the circumstances.

"The upshot of it was that I called a friend at one of the big firms, explained the situation, and asked him to find out what agency his firm used."

The friend did as asked.

"We hired the second person who came in, a forty-year-old woman who had been a legal stenographer, quit to get married and have children, and wanted to get back in business. She didn't care a hoot for the way the office looked—said her kids made a lot worse mess in the house—and after a week or so of practice her skills were perfect. She's still with us, by the way. When we got big enough to hire more people we used the same agency, with equally good results."

What keeps inferior agencies in business? Probably employers who, unlike the young lawyers, are willing to settle for third or fourth best—and employees who will do the same. Maybe the agencies figure they deserve each other.

Can You Type? | *chapter IV*

*Tremendous demand for secretaries—Not every-
one wants to be a secretary—Why some do—
What makes a good one—Secretarial and Speedwriting schools.*

At a Christmas party in the offices of a well-known advertising
agency a young art assistant struck up a conversation with an
attractive girl he'd never seen before.

"What do *you* do around here?" he asked her.

"Oh," she said vaguely, "it all depends. I write a little. I
help out with accounts. I co-ordinate interdepartmental business."

Puzzled, he questioned her further. It turned out she was
a secretary.

"Now why couldn't she have said so in the first place?"
he wondered later. "What's wrong with being a secretary? She

acted like she'd got some fatal disease! Did she think I'd stop talking to her if I knew what her job was?"

Maybe she did.

There seems to be something about the very word "secretary" that makes the female college graduate bristle. "Nobody's going to make *me* into a secretary!" she declares. "I didn't spend the last four years slaving just so I could wind up in somebody else's office taking shorthand!"

She will do anything to avoid the awful fate. How many times have they heard it in the employment agencies? "No, I can't type or take shorthand. Oh, no, I don't want to learn. Yes, I do want to go into advertising [or finance, or social work], but I don't want to be a secretary!"

As might be expected, what's hard to get is most sought after. If the shortage of good secretaries in New York City is large, and it is, the shortage of good college-educated secretaries is enormous. An employer who's lucky enough to find one is like a man who spots a Rembrandt in a junk shop: eager to tell the world about his find, yet certain that if he does someone else will pirate it away.

What makes the Rembrandts so few is that so many careerminded alumnae believe that a secretary's job is a dead end. As Shepherd Mead, author of *How to Succeed in Business* . . . , put it, "There is nothing so rare as the girl who likes to type. A really good typist can always get a job, because nobody wants to be one. The reason is that the only way to get ahead is to stop typing as soon as you can."

"There's such a need for secretaries," says a twenty-two-year-old job hunter, "that the minute a company finds out you can take shorthand you're dead. They don't even want to interview you for anything else."

This attitude is more typical of young women who are

serious about a business career than of those who came to the city hoping only to find a man to take them out of it. The latter are no less vehement in their determination to be "anything but a secretary," but with a difference.

"Those girls come in here looking for jobs when what they really want is a title to impress some guy," moaned the personnel manager of a woman's fashion magazine. "If I offer them a secretarial job, two to one they'll turn it down. But if it's labeled 'researcher' or 'trainee,' they'll jump at it.

"It's the exact same job with a different name."

This question of status bothers the determined career girl too, for other reasons. She's afraid that as a typist she may not be taken seriously by the people who matter. All too often, unfortunately, she's right. There are plenty of businessmen (and women) like the thirty-three-year-old merchandising executive who said, "My intellectual contact is with the staff, not the secretaries." Worse yet are the patronizers ("Some people here boss their assistants around for their own power needs. Not me. I don't like being authoritarian to secretaries").

No wonder if a college-trained secretary working under these conditions resents both her superiors and her job. Personal relations in business are complicated enough, she maintains, without having to deal from somebody else's marked deck.

Still, it all depends on the people, and for every career-minded college girl who shuns the typewriter there is an older woman who swears by it. New York City has thousands of women who hold responsible executive positions, and two out of every three started as secretaries. It would seem—contrary to the "dead-end" school of thought—that if a girl really wants to go places there is no better place to begin.

If, however, a girl makes a bad secretary, she will seldom

make a good executive. Every one of the personal attributes important in a vice president is at least as important in his right-hand girl. When the Katharine Gibbs School queried employers as to what they looked for in a secretary, traits most often mentioned were: native intelligence, adaptability, good personal appearance, technical excellence, and agreeable personality. In its student handbook Katharine Gibbs makes a particular point of the last: "A secretary should be pleasant and cheerful. She is often depended upon to maintain the morale of the office." In other words, leave the grouchiness to the boss. He's earned it.

Many executives mentioned "loyalty" among the qualities of a good secretary. Some put it right up at the top of the list. There is nothing more infuriating to an employer—or more damaging to an organization—than a private secretary who brings company affairs into public domain.

In 1959 the director of research at a chemical company in a small town hired a confidential secretary, a graduate of a nearby junior college. Six months after she went to work for him he had a phone call from a worried stockholder. "Just between us, Fred, is it true that you're giving up on that new cotton process?" asked the man. "Word's around that it hasn't worked out like the company thought. Tell me it's true and I'll unload my shares today."

The surprised executive promptly denied the rumor, which was false, but his friend sold anyway, precipitating a general sell-off, in the area, of the company's stock. It took weeks for the dismayed firm to track the rumor down to its source: the research director's new secretary.

She had complained to her boy friend, who told his father —the local dentist—that her boss got grumpy every time there was business relating to the research in progress. The town chewed over this phenomenon with predictable results.

The secretary was lucky to get off with a warning never again to discuss *anything* pertaining to company business, no matter how trivial it might seem. By the time she began to suspect the real reason behind her boss's grouchiness—he was worried about being transferred several hundred miles away to supervise one phase of the new operation—the damage had been done.

Loyalty to the employer is just as vital as loyalty to the firm. An executive secretary may disagree with every decision her boss makes, but she is duty bound to support him in front of other workers. No one can undermine the workings of a company so subtly or so swiftly as the girl who is the only link between higher-ups and employees.

One case in which an ad man lost his job after fifteen years' service involved just such a backbiting secretary. At thirty-six, the man, Mr. O., had held a succession of key jobs in a large New York agency, finally rising to become the youngest vice president in the firm's history. This fact in itself was enough to make him an object of some resentment among older co-workers; besides, as the agency's personnel manager tells the story, many people thought him arrogant, inconsiderate of underlings, and a perfectionist who demanded impossibly high standards of work from his staff.

On the other hand Mr. O. arrived early, left late, and drove no one so hard as himself. Even those who disliked him the most admitted that he deserved to be where he was.

Not surprisingly, this man had trouble getting along with his secretaries. After four had requested transfers in a period of a little over two years, the firm assigned him Miss R., a young woman who was "every bit as ornery as he," on the theory that two such difficult people, if they didn't murder each other the first day, might turn out to be ideally suited.

For some time all went well and the personnel manager congratulated himself on a perfect match. Actually, however, while boss and secretary made a good working team, they detested each other—only Mr. O. let off his feelings in frequent outbursts of invective while Miss R., possibly recognizing a master, kept hers bottled up.

One Friday while he was at lunch a call came in from one of the agency's top accounts, requesting that he get in touch with them. Miss R. left the message among others on his desk. It happened that her boss did not get back to the office that afternoon, and the call was not returned until the following Monday.

Later in the week the client informed the firm that its account was being transferred to another agency. No reason was given for the action.

Another of the company's vice presidents took it upon himself to find out what had gone wrong. As events were later reconstructed, he heard from his own private secretary, who got it from a research assistant, who had had it straight from Miss R., that Mr. O.'s failure to return the Friday phone call on the same day must have been in some way responsible.

Negligence on the part of Mr. O. seemed out of character, but he was so generally disliked that people who heard the story were only too ready to believe it. As the only explanation, however flimsy, anyone could offer for the loss of a good account, it was duly passed on to the company's president.

In advertising, when accounts go, men usually go too—sometimes with little reason and less cause. The unpleasant but efficient Mr. O. was fired.

Not long afterward the real reason for the client's switch

became obvious. He had a daughter—the daughter had a fiancé—and the son-in-law-to-be worked for the other agency.

No wonder so many employers stress loyalty.

Private secretaries interviewed in a downtown investment-banking firm had their own ideas about what makes a Tessie Typist a Della Street. Fourteen college graduates among them had, with one exception, majored in either economics or math, and the lone history major had worked in a bank for two summers before graduation.

"There's nothing so silly as a college girl's taking a job in a field she doesn't know anything about," said one young woman. "If you have a basic knowledge of the business, at least your four years will have meant something. That doesn't mean I think an economics major who hated every minute of it ought to go into finance just because she had the training. Interest is important too."

Just how important was illustrated by a twenty-three-year-old Oberlin graduate working in the same firm as a typist. Music was her passion, but after an unremunerative year spent composing and arranging she had gone to secretarial school. On the strength of her new skills and her college degree, the insurance firm started her off as secretary to a junior executive. Shortly after she began her boss left the firm, and while waiting for a new one she was "temporarily" assigned to the typists' pool with no reduction in pay. There she has remained.

"I know I ought to say something to somebody," she confessed, "but the salary's the same so it really doesn't matter what I do. In fact I'm probably better off where I am. This way at least I don't have to be involved in the 'thinking' side— I can just type off what they hand me without thinking about it. When I was somebody's secretary I had a lot more responsibility and they expected me to know figures and statistics and such. I guess I never took much trouble to learn. Banking is the most *boring* business!"

"Oh, yes, I know the girl," said a woman in the personnel department. "We thought highly of her when she began here; a college graduate, after all, with secretarial training—but her work was terribly lackadaisical. We made an exception for her, hoping she might improve, when we put her in the pool at a secretary's pay, but it doesn't seem to be working out and I understand they're planning to let her go as soon as things slow down. It's too bad. A nice enough girl, but absolutely no interest in the business."

Most B.A.s are wise enough to look for work in fields they like. They don't become secretaries because they enjoy taking shorthand. This is probably the major difference between the college-educated secretary and those without degrees. The latter, in most cases, don't particularly care where they work as long as the job pays well and offers good security.

A survey made by a metropolitan employment agency bears this out. "What is your first consideration in looking for a job?" they asked. Non-college graduates answered: 1) Salary; 2) Security; and 3) Benefits. College girls sought 1) Field; 2) Salary; and 3) Chance of Advancement. "Creativity"— which the agency did not even offer as a choice on its non-college survey—was a close fourth.

In view of this it is not surprising that firms having some connection with art, music, or literature employ a much higher percentage of graduates as secretaries than do those in more prosaic fields. "Creative" organizations demand more in a secretary than just the ability to punctuate, spell, and type. She is often called upon to read a manuscript, revise a collage, attend an audition, and contribute intelligent criticism when and where it's needed. Fully aware that the jobs they have to offer are the kind college girls want, these firms can afford to stint a little on salaries. A beginning secretary in an art gallery can expect about 70 to 75 dollars a week. Some large manufacturing firms offer nearly half again as much.

The real loser in the race for talent is not the XYZ paperbag company so much as its house organ. Young women who look for creative work look first for creative organizations, and often prefer a relatively routine clerical job in a prestige firm to more challenging work in a non-creative field.

"What my job lacks in imagination, it makes up in the chance to be around imaginative people," said a typist in a television production studio. "Every day there's something new to talk about. It really keeps you on your toes. I was never much interested in current events, for example, till I came here. Now I read two papers a day and *Time* every week. I have to, if I don't want to look dumb. The funny thing is, I enjoy it. I don't think I'll ever not keep up with the news again."

"When you have a job like mine," declared Suzanne Levin, a secretary-junior copywriter at an electrical-appliances firm, "you have to either be in love with irons and toasters or you have to look outside for intellectual stimulation. I took the job because I didn't want to waste time working my way up slowly in an ad agency. I'm not saying I did the wrong thing, understand. From the long-range point of view it was right, because in another year I'll have enough copywriting experience to get a better job in a different place.

"If only I had more in common with the people here it would be fine, but there are only two copywriters and nearly everyone else seems to have gone to business or accounting school. So far as I'm concerned, they speak a different language."

The girl who has a liberal-arts education and works in an office where others do not must be prepared to adapt or be unhappy. One of Suzanne Levin's co-workers said she was "silent and supercilious"; another thought her "stuck-up." "After all," he said, "most of us know a lot more about the business end of this company than she'll ever know. We were trained for this; she wasn't. But she's never seemed interested in talking business with the rest of us, and we mostly don't talk about much else in the office. This is a very business-minded place. We go to movies and theater and things just like anybody else, but we don't discuss it during working hours. She probably thinks we're a bunch of cultural clods."

What Suzanne Levin lacks in adaptability, Harriet Maxe has. She too felt it would be better to compromise and gain experience than hold out for exactly the right job, and following her '62 graduation from Pembroke she became girl Friday at a civil-service publication. Her job involves everything from typing out long lists of successful applicants for state employment to composing short paragraphs of birth, death, and retirement announcements. She also answers phones, proofreads, fetches coffee, assists the make-up editor, and takes the finished product down to the printer once a month.

"I don't meet famous authors," Harriet says, "but I do learn what publishing's all about. In a job like this with a small staff there are endless opportunities. It may not be the most creative job in New York, but there aren't many places I could write something one day and watch the printers set it up the day after. I think if I had to, I could probably set a page myself by now.

"When I first started here, I knew even less about civil

service than I did about publishing. But you either have to learn or—" She paused. "Well, I suppose you don't *have* to learn. But if you didn't, think how much less interesting it would be. This way I at least understand what the phone calls are about, and I can leave intelligent messages and be able to discuss problems with people who wander in if there's nobody else here. In fact I'm almost beginning to think I may stay in civil service—not even necessarily publishing, but maybe some other branch."

Harriet's boss, a woman, couldn't say too many nice things about her. "One of the most intelligent, unassuming, hardworking girls we've ever had," she raved. "When she began here, I was very much on guard for the slightest sign of a negative attitude—far more than I would have been with a girl who hadn't gone to college—but she's never refused to do anything anyone asked. She has a fine career ahead."

Harriet Maxe taught herself touch typing before she left college, but she is an exception. The vast majority of college women spend four years hunt-and-pecking their way through term papers. Liberal-arts colleges do not give courses in typing and shorthand—that's not what they're there for—and if they did, few girls would take them. "If I decide to be a secretary I can always go to secretarial school after college," is the general attitude.

When the decisive moment comes, however, not very many do attend secretarial schools. In the Smith '58 class of 497 girls, 11 went on to secretarial school, which is about average for a liberal-arts institution.

One thing a good secretarial school does do is provide job insurance. At the Katharine Gibbs School, the girl who goes because she sincerely wants to be a topnotch secretary, and the girl who goes because she's already had her trip to Europe, isn't interested in an advanced degree, and can't think what else to do, both have an assured future in the business world, assuming they graduate, from the day they enter. If landing a good secretary is like finding an oyster in Central Park, then landing a KG girl is like finding a pearl inside.

Katharine Gibbs's free placement service has approximately 500 jobs on file in its office any day of the year, just waiting for girls to graduate and fill them. To protect all concerned, the school maintains a hard-and-fast "six months' rule" for new graduates. A girl who takes a job must keep it for at least six months or forfeit her right to use the placement service again. This is one reason why Gibbs girls are so in demand: employers can be fairly certain that they won't decide to leave after a few weeks on the job.

Katharine Gibbs, with branches in several Eastern cities, is the heavy favorite among liberal-arts graduates who take secretarial training. It is not cheap. Tuition at Gibbs costs the prospective secretary (or, more often, her father) about 1000 dollars a year. Not every girl can afford that much, nor does everyone want to attend a year-round school. For the girl in a hurry and/or a financial hole, there are any number of good Speedwriting, stenographic, and business schools that grant degrees after a minimum six-week training period at much lower cost. Ninety-nine per cent of the students in these courses are not college graduates, but a girl who is, like one Cornell alumna who began taking an eight-month course and completed it with distinction in three months, can usually work at her own pace.

Time and money are usually well spent on secretarial schools. They pay off in increased salaries for increased skills and, in the case of the better ones, in that they provide the kind of blanket coverage of the job market that a girl could never get on her own. A good job often begins far from the office.

The secretarial day from nine to five—Bosses
they like and those they don't like—Jobs ditto—
Office problems, business and otherwise: how
they handle their bosses, covering up for them,
et cetera.

Six minutes to 9 on a bright May morning. Anita Van
Ermann tucked the *Times* and the *Tribune* under her arm,
shifted her weight against a sudden forward press, and let
herself be carried along to the open rear door of a Madison
Avenue bus.

Emerging, she peered at her watch. The window of "Max
Schling, Seedsmen" caught her attention momentarily; then,
with an appreciative glance at a seersucker suit striding past,
she began walking south toward Fifty-first Street.

Eight fifty-seven. Anita entered an express elevator, greeted
the operator, and arrived with a stomach-lifting jump at the

nineteenth floor. Selecting a key from her bag, she picked up the mail and unlocked the double doors of Willis, Hammerman, Realty and Estate Agents. She flicked on the lights and made a quick tour of the windows, snapping up shades as she went.

Nine sharp, and down the hall other doors began to open. The office of Willis, Hammerman, a three-room suite, contains a small reception room with a desk, water cooler, and two armless swivel chairs; a conference room crowded with file cabinets and a table nearly the room's length with six hard-backed chairs ranged haphazardly around it; and a third room, largest of all, which the partners share. Bookcases line the walls here, and two desks sit facing each other across an expanse of dark carpet, each with a matching leather-padded chair.

Anita, having opened the windows in the inner rooms—the reception room is windowless—looked critically at the desk tops. One bore coffee stains. She found a sponge in a cabinet, wet it from the cooler in the front room, and cleaned up the desk. Then she sharpened ten pencils, putting four on each partner's desk and two on her own; brought both men's desk calendars up to date, opened the mail, threw out several circulars and laid the rest on the desks, and sat down to check the wording of the firm's ads in the *Times*' real-estate section.

At 9:20 the phone rang. "Willis, Hammerman, may I help you?" It was Mr. Hammerman, who had stopped for a haircut and would be a little late. Had Mrs. Behrens called about the lot in Queens? "Not so far." Good. He'd be in shortly.

Finding an error in an ad offering for sale a two-family brownstone house in Chelsea, Anita called the *Times*. The typo would be corrected in tomorrow's paper. She checked the

Tribune, glanced at its society page, and called the drugstore downstairs. "Orange juice, two regular coffees, a plain Danish, and one tea."

She unlocked a drawer and swung her typewriter out from beneath. Typewriter and desk were attached. From the middle drawer she took a stenographer's pad and began to transcribe dictation. "Dear Mr. Marks," she typed. "The property offered by you for sale on March 31, 1963 . . ."

She typed on steadily. At 9:50 Clarence Willis, Jr., thirty-seven, entered. "Anita, hi. How was the weekend?" "Lou's at the barber, Clarry. He'll be late." He walked through to the partners' room. "Forget to order my breakfast?"

She called the drugstore again; the boy was on his way up. When he came she paid him, adding a tip, from a petty-cash box in the main office; put juice, pastry, and coffee in front of Mr. Willis and tea on Mr. Hammerman's desk, and carried her own coffee back to the reception room.

As a student at Wheaton College, Anita Van Ermann, of Lowell, Massachusetts, majored in government. Engaged early in her junior year to a boy at Dartmouth's Amos Tuck School of Business, she had never given much thought to a career, vaguely supposing that she might take a temporary job in "international relations" until children came.

Two months before graduation and the scheduled date of her wedding, the engagement was broken. Around the same time an uncle died, leaving Anita a house and two acres of land in Great Barrington, Massachusetts. "At the time," she says, "I was pretty desperate for something to occupy my mind so I wouldn't think too much, and then this house thing came along. We—my family—decided I should put it up for sale. It was sold to a woman from New York, and that's how

I met Mr. Willis, who was her agent. The negotiations, the title search and so forth, were very interesting. When Mr. Willis found out I was graduating soon and didn't have a job he asked me if I'd ever thought of being a secretary because his own girl was leaving to get married."

The firm paid Anita's tuition for an eight-week secretarial course, and in September she began work.

The telephone rang again. "Willis, Hammerman. Oh, good morning, Mrs. Behrens. Mr. Hammerman was a little delayed getting here this morning. Will you speak with Mr. Willis? . . . Of course. I'll have Mr. Hammerman call you as soon as he gets in."

She went on typing. At 10:20 the intercom buzzed. She pressed a button beneath her desk. "Yes, sir? . . . Be right in."

Mr. Willis wanted to discuss a lease. "Let's have your thinking on this, Anita. Mrs. Clay, the one who's taking the O'Hare apartment, wants us to give her a new sink. According to records O'Hare got a sink from the building four years ago. Mrs. Clay says it works fine but it looks like hell. From a woman's point of view, would you say she'd be satisfied if we give her a good enamel job on the old sink? Or do you think she'll be after us again next year, wanting a new one?"

"I'd say the enamel would make her just as happy, Clarry. A sink should still be in good shape after only four years, and after it's sprayed it'll look brand-new. I wouldn't complain if it was me."

"That's what I thought too. Thanks, old girl. Will you take care of the records, please?"

While she was filing the O'Hare papers in one of the cabinets in the board room Anita came across a folder that had been incorrectly filed. She glanced through it with interest (at the bottom of one letter, Mr. Hammerman had written: "Clarry—tenants like this we can do without") and put it in its proper place.

Ten forty-five. Lou Hammerman, a heavy-set man in his early forties, arrived. "Morning, Anita. Unavoidably delayed. Mrs. Behrens call? . . . Get her for me, will you, like a good girl?" He passed through and could be heard greeting his partner inside.

As Anita was dialing the number, the buzzer rang. Mr. Hammerman wanted her to listen in on the extension as he talked and transcribe the call. Later, perhaps, her notes might be needed. ("That's not what we agreed on over the phone, Mrs. Behrens. Now I have here an exact record of our conversation . . .")

She picked up a pencil and dialed again. "Mrs. Behrens? . . . I have Mr. Hammerman for you now. One moment, please." She pressed the intercom. "Mrs. Behrens on two."

For the next five minutes she wrote rapidly, her telephone pressed between ear and shoulder as she turned pages. Mrs. Behrens had heard a rumor that the land she wanted to subdivide was about to be zoned against small plots. Not true, as far as Mr. Hammerman knew, but he would ask around. The land was close to water. What about hurricane and flood insurance? He could put her in touch with a good agent, complete coverage at low rates, nothing to worry about. Anita took it all down. When the conversation ended she waited to hear the click of both receivers being replaced; then hung up her own.

The buzzer sounded almost immediately. "Let me have those notes as soon as you can, Anita," said Lou Hammerman's voice. She took her correspondence from the typewriter, inserted a piece of yellow onionskin paper, and typed up the shorthand she had taken.

Eleven thirty-five. Anita sat back in her chair and picked up the phone. "Molly Conley, please. Molly? . . . Hi. . . . Anita. How was the weekend? . . . No, nothing interesting. You going out for lunch? . . . Fine, love to. . . . Oh, the usual place. See you then."

She looked up as an elderly man entered.

"May I help you? Oh, it's Mr. Rodansky, isn't it? Have you an appointment, sir?" She pressed the intercom. "Mr. Rodansky to see you, Mr. Willis." Pause. "Will you take a seat, Mr. Rodansky? He'll be right with you."

She smiled. The visitor seated himself gingerly on the only other chair and smiled back.

A minute later the buzzer sounded under her desk. "Yes, sir? Surely." She got up. "Will you come this way, please?" She led Mr. Rodansky into the conference room, where Clarence Willis waited. Anita shut the door behind them and poked her head into the partners' office. Mr. Hammerman was gazing out the window.

"Anything you need, Lou? I'm going out to lunch pretty soon." Lou Hammerman asked her to pick him up a tongue sandwich on the way back to the office.

At noon Anita went in again. "I'm leaving now. See you at one."

After a quick stop in the ladies' room she was off. Madison Avenue, jammed with people hurrying to meet other people, sped by in a blur of straw hats, gay cotton print dresses, intent faces. Two blocks down she turned a corner and halted before Hicks restaurant.

Molly Conley greeted her. "Hey, you look winded. You run all the way?"

They took the last two seats at the counter and ordered cottage-cheese salads and iced tea. The waitress smiled at them. "Hi, girls."

Anita took out a cigarette. "My first today. Did I tell you I'm giving up smoking? Gradually. How's old Finky?"

Her friend began to discuss the latest foibles of her boss.

He had given her fourteen pages of dictation at 4:30 Friday. This morning at 10 A.M. he wanted to know why it hadn't been typed yet.

He had sent her out last week to buy him suspenders; then made her change them on her lunch hour because he didn't like the color.

He warned her at least twice a day not to discuss office politics with other people's secretaries.

He criticized her typing.

She went on, while Anita nodded sympathetically. "I don't know why you take it, Molly. If I were you I'd look around for something else."

"Oh, I probably make it sound worse then it is. Pete's just one of the chronic gripers. I'm pretty used to him by now."

They ordered desserts: pecan pie and a cherry sundae. Lunch came to 1.40 apiece and each left a 20-cent tip.

"Time for a quick look in Saks?" They hurried up to Fifth and across. In the store, well-dressed older women strolled slowly; younger ones clutched packages and peered at their watches. Molly lingered at the handbag counter. Anita watched the crowd.

"Oh, Lord, I almost forgot. I've got to pick something up for Lou. I better leave you here, Mol. Call me."

She got back to the office just as Mr. Rodansky was leaving. "Some long conference, Clarry." "Some long-winded guy," muttered her employer. "I'm meeting Jack Burton for lunch, Anita. You know where to get me if you need me."

He left. Anita gave Lou Hammerman his sandwich and settled at her desk. She finished transcribing the dictation begun earlier and answered two phone calls, passing one on to Mr. Hammerman and telling the other that yes, the deed was in the mail and should arrive by tomorrow. Then she straightened out the chairs in the conference room and started the *Times* crossword puzzle. So far, it had been a slow day.

Two P.M. Lou Hammerman came into the outer room and peered over Anita's shoulder. "Reverse," he said, pointing. "Twenty-two across. Reverse." He picked up a pencil and jotted down an address in the Bronx. "Speaking of reverse, Anita, you can do me a big favor, if you will. Take my car, it's in the lot, and run on up to this place. There's a Miss Smith in apartment 4B complaining about her painting job. She says the plaster's cracking in the kitchen. Super says there's nothing wrong with the job. He suspects she just changed her mind about the color and wants us to do it over for free. See what you think, will you? I'd go myself but with Clarry out I'd better stay here. Let me have a memo on it."

It was nearly four when Anita returned. She sat down at once to the typewriter. "Memo from Miss Van Ermann to Mr. Hammerman," she typed. "Re kitchen painting 4B (L. T. Smith), 411 F.D.R. Drive.

"The super must be blind," she typed, "or maybe just near-sighted. Inspection showed plaster cracking on the ceiling, behind the sink, and near the window. Nothing very bad as yet, but the job was only done two weeks ago and is sure to get worse fast. There's been trouble with the plumbing in the apartment above, which probably accounts for it.

"Recommendation: We should give the tenant a new paint job."

She filed a carbon of the memo in a Manila folder marked "Smith, L.T.," and dropped the original in the "in" basket on Mr. Hammerman's desk.

Mr. Willis called to her on her way out. "Hate to do it this late, Anita, but I'd better give you some notes on the Rodansky thing while it's still fresh in my mind. It won't take too long."

She followed him into the conference room, leaving Mr. Hammerman at his desk, reading her memo and shaking his head.

The Rodansky conference had been productive. As his agent, the firm of Willis, Hammerman was to receive 4400 dollars upon transferring title to his house. The fee, fifteen per cent of the selling price, would be paid in four quarterly installments. Anita wrote briskly.

At 5:10 Clarence Willis leaned back in his chair and sighed. "That's about it, old girl. Send a carbon to Rodansky."

She tucked her notes under her typewriter roller and swung the machine out of sight. Over her shoulder, to the two men within: "I'm off now. See you tomorrow." From the inner office came Lou Hammerman's voice. "See you, Anita. Thanks for the Smith thing."

At 5:15, Anita locked her desk and left.

The secretary's day can be sedentary or physically exhausting; routine or full of surprises. It all depends on what goes into it. Start with certain ingredients. Interest. Ability to handle the work. A good boss. Innumerable other factors help make the difference between a job that makes a girl look forward to Friday and one that has her impatient for Monday to come, but these three are essential.

The first two, interest and ability, are the secretary's own problem. If she doesn't like the field she's in or hasn't the proper skills to do the work she has no one to blame but herself. The third, a good boss, is more complicated because it's beyond her control and a matter of sheer luck. The man who seemed such a lamb at the interview could be a bear once work starts—or maybe a wolf.

What makes a good boss? A consensus of 200 secretaries in the metropolitan area turned up almost as many different opinions, but one quality that many girls think essential is an amiable disposition. If a man is a nice guy, they say, he'll probably have most of the other traits they look for.

Also mentioned by a majority, in one way or another, was fairness. The man who plays office favorites, or puts the blame for his own errors on his secretary, or encourages employees to report to him on each other's mistakes earns neither the respect nor the liking of his staff.

Girls look for fairness outside the office as well as in.

"I didn't exactly dislike my last boss personally so much," said a secretary in a medical-insurance program. "I just disliked the way things were shaping up. He was a doctor with a Park Avenue practice and very wealthy patients. I thought he was unethical in his dealings with them. Even after people didn't need any more treatment he'd keep them coming back for checkups and such. He was just trying to get as much money as possible. I said something about it to him once and he told me it made people feel better if they thought their doctor was concerned enough with their health to want to see them for frequent consultations—and anyway, he said, they could afford it."

She quit the job, which paid 90 dollars a week, and took another at 5 dollars less.

"I have a strongly developed sense of business ethics. I probably got it from working with that guy."

No amount of interest in a job can make up for a bad boss. On the other hand, a good boss often compensates for a bad job.

In the correspondence department of a record firm, Sally Howes and Barbara Rosenthal, both Oberlin '61, work as secretaries. Their desks stand side by side in one corner of a crowded and, in summer, stiflingly hot room. Their job is to compose and type replies in answer to the many inquiries and requests the firm receives each day ("Dear Miss Roberts, We are sending under separate cover the recording you have requested . . ."; "Dear Mr. Brown, In answer to your query, Frank Sinatra has never made any recordings on our label . . .").

After a week on the job, the two said, they had the system down pat and could "write the letters in our sleep." Others in the office—a bookkeeper, two file clerks, and a receptionist —also did routine work. "The only thing that keeps us all from going stir crazy," said Barbara, "is that we have one of the greatest supervisors in the business. He's a young, very cheerful guy, to begin with. He has us laughing most of the time. He gets all the records before they're released and he keeps a phonograph at his desk so there's always music playing. Sometimes he'll jump up on his desk and do the twist, or come over to one of us and ask us to dance. Or he'll pick up a letter and say something like, 'Dear Mrs. Smith, Of all the inane requests we've ever had yours is the jerkiest.'

"It might sound like we don't get much done around here, but it's just the opposite. All of us work a lot harder than we would if he wasn't around. Sometimes everybody in the office gets through with the day's work around 3:30 and then we all leave together for a drink.

"I know my job isn't much, but at least I enjoy it."

Secretaries agree that a cheerful atmosphere is a great morale booster. Only sometimes, they say, togetherness can be carried a little too far.

A man's secretary, it has been said, probably knows him better than any woman in the world, including his wife. There was the *New Yorker* cartoon some time ago of the distressed husband saying to his wife, "My secretary doesn't understand me!" The trouble is that some men want more "understanding" from their secretaries than the office situation allows—so they try to make contact after hours.

The problem of the overfriendly employer is about as old as the twentieth century, in the early years of which "female secretaries" first began entering the labor market in meaningful numbers. From their mothers, from their colleges, from their books, they heard the same storm warnings. A 1914 alert came through loud and clear.

"The intelligent girl will not be unduly suspicious, but the moment that she detects a tendency in the conduct of any person with whom she works to pass the line of friendly business relationship, she should encase herself in her armor of true womanliness and by her alert, energetic attention to her work, discourage with finality any such overtures. If an icy, detached manner will not check the confidences of one's employer . . . she should promptly seek other employment."[1]

Nowadays the signals are a little blurred. "The secretary should not seek advancement . . . by attempting to influence

[1] Mary A. Laselle, *The Young Woman Worker*, Boston: Pilgrim Press, 1914.

her superior by any means other than the merit of her work," pointedly advises the Katharine Gibbs rule book.

But it has nothing to advise the girl whose superior is trying to influence *her*.

"He's always wanting me to work late and then 'go someplace for a drink.' I know what *that* means."

"My roommate's thinking of clearing out because her boss keeps making passes at her."

"Mister X thinks I'm here for his personal pleasure. It never seems to occur to him that I'm just trying to do a job."

Some girls, of course, welcome the boss's overtures. But for every one who does there seem to be two who do not.

"I have no personal problems with my boss—not any more, anyway," said a twenty-seven-year-old Westerner from Arizona State University. "I don't say we weren't attracted to one another; intellectually very much so, in the beginning. He is forty and married.

"The first couple of months he took me to lunch a few times and sent me little notes, the kind you could interpret however you wanted to. About three months after I started he made it plain that he was interested in having an affair. He suggested we start 'dating.'

"I said I wasn't interested and that he wanted to get me involved in something that could be permanently upsetting. I said even if for the moment I *did* want to get involved, it wasn't for me.

"He tried over a period of two–three weeks to persuade me, then stopped. Since then I've realized it really would have been a disaster. Now he just says things like, 'Gee, that's a nice dress,' and gives me a few soulful glances. Rather flattering and fun.

"Things have been a little difficult since all this happened, as you can imagine. Since he's my immediate supervisor I see him a lot. I act very lighthearted about it and try and ignore it in terms of our office relationship. He has never hinted at it since."

One secretary thought that out-of-towners run into this problem more than New York girls—perhaps, she suggests, because their bosses suspect them of leaving their restrictions back where they came from. Others say no, it depends wholly on the girl herself.

"I have never had the slightest trouble with the men on the staff," said one. "I graduated quite young, at nineteen [she is now twenty-five] and came here very naïve, and people tend to retain first impressions, I've noticed. So now I'm still the sweet girl graduate and they're very helpful still, and sweet and nice. I won't say I don't deliberately act dumb sometimes to keep up the impression."

"I wish men would realize that not every out-of-towner leaves her morals with her mother," said another girl. "Sure, I've had men say to me, 'Oh, you've got your own apartment?' with that look you can't miss. I may be living away from home, but I'm still me, aren't I?"

One very attractive out-of-towner left job after job because of unwanted male attentions and finally wound up working for a woman, which seems to be the logical solution for girls who are really sincere about not wanting to be "bothered."

The girls who work for the trade magazine *Today's Secretary*, read almost exclusively by members of the profession, have at one time or another heard all these problems and any others you might care to name. Somewhat on the order of *Seventeen* and *Business Week* combined, *Today's Secretary* gives hints on clothes, shorthand, cosmetics, paycheck deductions, how to get a job, how to get a husband, and how to handle dates—the spelling of them, that is. One special problem of being a secretary for *Today's Secretary* is the letters that come in from *other* secretaries asking for help with *their* problems. The magazine's staff never knows what will pop up next in the mail.

> My boss is in the hospital. He hates candy and flowers, and doesn't smoke or drink. What shall I get him?
>
> Whenever there's a coffee break, one girl takes her coffee and goes in the boss's office and closes the door. Gossip is starting. Should I say something?
>
> I never know what to do with mail when my boss has people with him. Should I take it in or wait?

And, for a question that none but the asker could answer, the all-time favorite of *Today's Secretary's* secretaries:

> My boss and I share an office. Is it right for people to just walk in or should they knock?

His Right-hand Girl | *chapter VI*

Previous training—From typist to executive secretary: the way up—Secretaries in various industries: different surroundings and salaries— The importance of being indispensable— Bosses' opinions.

"You might not believe that a girl could graduate from college and not only not know *what* she wanted to do, but not want to do *anything*," said Betty Beekley, "but you're looking at one right this minute."

She waved her hand toward the spacious office where, beyond the windows, steel and glass buildings shone luminous in the late-afternoon sun. From near the door came the steady rattle of typing.

"Miss Misfit of the class of 1957, and look where I wind up!"

Where she wound up is on the eleventh floor of a tower-

ing Park Avenue office building. The firm she works for as an
executive secretary, with two assistants and an office of her
own, is an import-export company occupying the ninth, tenth,
and eleventh floors.

Betty Beekley is a slim brunette of twenty-five with a junior-
college education and a salary of 145 dollars per week. She
has been with the same firm for seven years, ever since graduation, beginning on the lowest rung of the secretarial ladder
as a 55-dollar-a-week typist in the office pool. What happened
to her on her way to her present position is fairly typical of
what an aspiring executive secretary can expect.

"To begin with, I had no ambition whatever. Absolutely
zero. It was lucky I'd taken a typing course at school because
it was just about the only useful thing I knew how to do. At
college I didn't give a thought to work, a career, anything. I
spent the summer after graduation sitting around on the
beach, waiting, I suppose, for some man to come and find me.

"Then all of a sudden it was September and no college to
go back to—not that I wanted to, anyway. My family started
making unsubtle hints like, 'Look at all the wonderful jobs in
the paper,' and, 'Isn't it grand, the opportunities in business
for girls nowadays?' It took me a few weeks just to get up the
energy to go looking for a job. I must have been the most
unenthusiastic beginner they ever had here.

"This was the first place I looked. I had a list of about six
possibilities clipped from the *Times*, all of them for receptionists or typists. I started with this one because it was
closest to home.

"I liked the surroundings right away. Look around downstairs. It's lovely. And I must have made a pretty good impression because they hired me on the spot. I'd had about as
much training in typing as the others, though most of them

knew more about what was expected of you in business than
I did. As far as I remember, none of the typists had gone to
secretarial school. A girl who has usually gets to start right in
as a secretary, at least in this firm. There was one other girl
from college and me, and the rest—there were about thirty in
all, in the pool—had taken commercial courses in high school.
For most of us it was our first job.

"There I was, Betty Beekley, Girl Typist. We all sat in one
big room—air conditioned, thank heaven—and did the routine
typing that nobody else could be bothered with. Notice of
shipments, and so forth. We had a woman supervisor who
would give out work at the beginning of the day. When you
finished, you'd hand it to her and she'd check for spelling
errors, neatness, et cetera. There was a tremendous volume of
work—all thirty of us were almost always kept busy all the
time—and if you made too many mistakes you were out.
They couldn't afford to waste time training a girl properly.
It was kind of like a factory assembly line; you had to produce a certain amount of work in eight hours or else. A girl
who had to do a thing twice to get it right didn't last long.

"I found it pretty easy work. Completely uncreative, of
course. Typing out form letters and other people's thoughts
doesn't give you much chance to think for yourself. The times
I liked best were when I was requisitioned as a substitute
secretary. They use people from the pool to fill in when a
regular secretary gets sick or goes on vacation. The only thing
was that I didn't know how to take shorthand, so when there
was something that involved dictation I got passed over.
Since then we've had Dictaphones installed in most of the
major executive offices and a few of the others, but at that
time we were still using womanpower.

"I think if it hadn't been for the need for more social contact I'd still be a typist. I guess different girls are motivated by different things to want to advance: more money, a more interesting job, or what have you. In my case it was just that I didn't have many friends among the girls in the pool. I got along well with the secretaries I'd met, but the organization has a pretty rigid pecking order—if you're a typist you have lunch with the typists; if you're a secretary, with the secretaries, and so on.

"Also there was the problem of men, or should I say no men. Unless you were called in to sub for a secretary you never saw a man all day. It was like college all over again, only worse because there at least we had men professors!

"After about six months I decided I liked the place well enough to want to stay but not well enough to stay a typist. So I came home one day and announced I was going to business school at night to learn to be a stenographer. My family nearly collapsed.

"I took an all-around course: how to take dictation, shorthand, orders, everything. I even gained thirty words a minute in my typing speed. Halfway through the course the woman supervisor here gave me an assignment where I had to take dictation and she told me the man told her I was fine.

"The whole thing gave me such a lift. It was around then that I started thinking maybe I wasn't such a good-for-nothing after all. I think they must have noticed the change at work, because near the end of my course the personnel people called me in and told me they'd been hearing good things about me, and that I should just keep it up and they'd watch me and I'd be hearing from them. After *that* I worked harder than ever.

"A week after I got my diploma I was promoted. Not to secretary, because that would have been too big a jump after just nine months on the job. They put me up one place to stenographer. That meant I was a kind of secretary's assistant, like the two I have now in the room outside. My salary was raised, I think it was 70 dollars a week, and I got moved up to the tenth floor.

"The job itself wasn't so very different from the one I'd had except that it involved shorthand and dictation. Stenographers here are responsible to secretaries, not to executives. My boss was secretary to an assistant treasurer in charge of our Belgian imports. We have branches in nine countries, by the way, and we do business with seventeen, including two of the new African nations where we have traveling representatives.

"I usually worked directly with the secretary. She and I shared an office. I took all my dictation from her, or I'd transcribe the shorthand she'd taken from him. I didn't see much of him unless she was out. The main difference, of course, was in the surroundings. Instead of being one among thirty girls, typing things that made no sense to me for a different department every hour, I was part of an office, and I got to know the routine of how that one department worked. For the first time I really felt I was working in an import-export firm and not, say, an insurance company. It makes a very big difference when you can feel that you're really needed, that it would take time to train somebody else to do the job you're doing and you couldn't be replaced just as easily by a typist who walked in off the street.

"Socially I was much happier too. My boss—the secretary —was a very nice older woman, and her boss was a sweet guy. The job kept me moving around a lot too. I forgot to tell you that as the junior person in the office I was expected to run all kinds of errands in the building—get coffee for the others and so on. I didn't mind it a bit because it gave me a chance to meet more people.

"At lunch I'd naturally talk to the other stenographers about what went on in their offices, and pretty soon I was starting to get a good over-all picture of how the firm functions. One girl might work with tariffs, another with contacts in foreign countries, another with payments, like me, another with American distributors—you see? I even started making sense on the subject of importing to my family. It got to a point I'd never thought I'd see: I really was interested in what I was doing. I don't say I loved my particular job, because after all it was still pretty much routine work, but at least there was the chance to learn the business.

"I was a stenographer for about a year. This company has a policy of routine promotion on a certain time basis; I think you're supposed to be a stenographer for two years. But they counted in the time I'd spent as a typist toward my promotion and made me a secretary without the extra year.

"They don't assign you to an executive right off. You start as a kind of 'junior secretary' working with junior executives. In some ways it's harder than being secretary to just one man, although the actual work load is about the same. I was assigned to a group of five trainees, or junior execs as we call them. Since they spend a lot of their time walking around various departments, seeing how different ones operate, they don't get too much time for regular dictation. But they are expected to remember what they see and what they're told, so I always went along on the observation rounds to take notes. This was really great as far as I was concerned. It gave me the chance to see the processes I'd heard about in action. Actually the company is very smart. It was training me right along with the trainees, because a secretary, no matter what department she winds up in, ought to know something about the workings of the others. When you're responsible to an executive you can really help him by knowing and understanding what's going on in other places, and you can't talk intelligently to someone else's secretary until you have a pretty clear idea of what her job's about. In other words, knowing the business is good for business.

"Another thing I learned in that job, which incidentally paid 85 dollars a week, was how to work under pressure. You can't imagine what chaos is till you're the only secretary to five frantic guys who have to turn in weekly reports on what they've learned. Every Friday I'd have to type up those five reports. The boys didn't dictate them, lucky for me, because there wouldn't have been enough hours in the day to take all that dictation and transcribe it too. They used to write their reports at home on Thursday nights and then my only problem was trying to decipher five sets of scribbles. But even doing *that* was a help to me later, believe it or not. I seldom have trouble reading anybody's handwriting any more, and we get some letters here that you wouldn't believe.

"The training program lasted six months. At the end of it I can honestly say I knew nearly everything there was to know about the firm, plus my typing and stenography were really pretty professional.

"When the six months were up, the five men were assigned to various jobs in other cities for field training. At this point I should have become a full secretary to an executive, but it happened that nobody needed a secretary just then. They gave me a choice of going back to the pool with first option as a substitute, or starting on a new group of trainees, while I waited for something to open up. I picked the pool. You might think that was crazy but I thought it might be fun for a

while to be typing letters and this time know what the letters
were about. But after a couple of days I'd had it. The old
routine was deadly after everything I'd been doing.

"I came awfully close to quitting then. In fact I remember
going up to Personnel and giving two-week notice. They were
very sympathetic about it all and very nice; said something
was sure to come up and I shouldn't leave just when I was
getting someplace, and to just have a little patience.

"As it happened, one of our vice presidents got transferred
abroad the very next week and they let him take his secretary
along. So that left two vacant jobs and, as far as I was concerned, an ideal setup with a brand-new boss. Any secretary
will tell you she'd rather break in with a new man than someone who's accustomed to his old secretary's doing things their
old way and wants everything to be exactly the same.

"My boss was brought in from Chicago to head up our New
York distribution department. He'd had plenty of experience
with distribution in Chicago, and I knew the New York
side well enough to be of some use, so together we made a
good team.

"I've been lucky with bosses right along. This one was no
different. A very jovial Midwesterner; a hard worker but fun
to work with. We hit it off beautifully.

"For a few weeks there were just the two of us in the office.
It took about that long to familiarize ourselves with the
routine and get to know the people in the department. As you
know, this is a tremendous organization with about 200 in
staff in New York alone. There were 15 people in all working
under my boss.

"After the get-acquainted period, when we started real work,
they sent me a stenographer all my own. That was when I
first had that 'I've-got-it-made' feeling. I used to drag her

name into conversations just so I could tell people, 'Well, Sally—that's my assistant—said thus and so.' It made me feel a kind of executive too, working under somebody but still having somebody else working under me. And I learned how to delegate responsibility, which was something I'd never had to do before.

"For example, say Jack—that's my boss—asked to find out what was holding up delivery of an order to one of our wholesale outlets. Something like that could be touchy. Maybe the firm hadn't paid us for the last shipment. Maybe the stuff got lost in transit. Maybe the overseas office slipped up and never sent it at all. Any number of possibilities had to be investigated, which meant asking questions.

"To avoid making enemies you have to be careful how you ask questions, always implying that of *course* you know it couldn't be *their* fault but perhaps they might have heard something that would give you a lead?

"As you can see, it's smart to be friendly with other secretaries, especially in an office the size of this one. My closest friends now are secretaries to executives. Outside the office we play bridge and go to movies and plays and have dinner together. When we're outside we usually make a conscious effort not to talk shop. But in the office we exchange a lot of information, so we can operate better. This helps with bosses—to know what's going on.

"It's important that other secretaries trust you, and that you don't 'sell' your information—'Let's trade rumors,' stuff like that. Some people like to know things just so they can feel important later on in spreading them around.

"About delegating responsibility. If I had to find out anything like that I'd always do it myself. It's best not to have the steno know *too* much because for one thing most of them don't have the same sense of loyalty secretaries do, and don't make the distinction between gossip that can come in handy and gossip that can hurt you. A stenographer's job should just involve the business side of business—shorthand, typing, taking dictation. I don't mean I made my steno do all the dirty work, just the overload. After all, a secretary is hired mainly for her skills. I guess knowing how to delegate responsibility really means knowing where to draw the line.

"As secretary to an executive I made 105 dollars a week, and earned it too. That was when I learned how to mix drinks and pour tea without slopping it over—all the social graces I'd never bothered to learn before. We had a constant stream of people coming in and I had to know what they drank, if they drank, how they wanted it mixed, milk or cream, whether they'd had lunch and if not what kind of sandwich to order—my brother said it sounded like I was a glorified Geisha girl.

"Also I had to watch my step talking to people on the phone—'developing the proper phone manner,' they call it. This wasn't too easy for me to learn because I get impatient if I don't catch on right away. Once someone called up; it was only about a month after I started, wanting to speak to Jack. I couldn't make out his name, he spoke with such a heavy accent. I kept trying to get him to spell it for me but he pronounced the letters so unintelligibly that I couldn't get anywhere. Finally I got so frustrated I told him Jack wasn't there. I came close to losing my job because the man called the president's office to complain and it turned out he was a big client of ours. Jack went to bat for me that time. He told them he really had been out, which he wasn't.

"After that happened I was very careful with incoming calls. I kept a list of people in the firm who speak foreign languages, and I had a list of how to say 'Do you speak (whatever it is)?'

in twenty languages. I went right down the list and when I got to the right one I'd transfer the call to whoever could understand it. It didn't happen too often, but better safe than sorry.

"I think that was the only time Jack had to cover up for me. I've had to do it for him fairly often. That's an important part of a secretary's job. Say he goes to lunch and is late getting back for a two-o'clock meeting in the office. Instead of standing around like a dope I'll say, 'Gentlemen, Mr. Carter has asked me to outline for you the background of this afternoon's conference,' and then I'll just stretch it out till he gets back. Of course it means I have to know what the background *is*.

"Sometimes a secretary has to take the blame for things even if she knows it's the boss's fault. You can't have the whole office thinking the boss is a goop. There was one girl here—she didn't last too long—who just couldn't get it through her head that she should let people think the boss's mistakes were hers. They used to talk about her at lunch. If her boss lost something, instead of saying, 'I must have misplaced it' she'd say, 'I told you that would happen if you didn't take care of things.' Right in front of everybody! Then if she did find whatever it was she'd go around saying, 'He's so absent-minded. What would he do without me?' When her stenographer had trouble transcribing something he'd written, this girl told her not to worry; he had the worst handwriting in the world and no one could be expected to read it.

"Needless to say, morale in that office was pretty low. I suppose people figure that if the boss is doing such a rotten job they can't be expected to do much more. Only it wasn't the boss. It was the secretary.

"Jack was head of New York distribution for three years. He's only about forty-three and everyone said he had a great future with the company. As far as I was concerned, that was just hunky-dory, because I'd gone as far as I could hope to go on my own. In this firm, once a girl becomes secretary to an executive—which is not the same as executive secretary—she's had it. From there on in, her progress, if there is any, depends on her boss. If he gets promoted to a really top job, she might go along with him.

"That's what happened to me. Jack got made head of the whole cross-country distribution setup, and I got promoted from just plain secretary to executive secretary. That means I have my own office with two in staff working for me and I make an excellent salary. Also, when Jack's away I'm allowed to make decisions in his name.

"I feel more secure in the job than I ever have before. Nobody's indispensable, but you try to come as close to it as you can. You hope to get to a point where your boss says, 'Betty, I don't know what I'd do without you.'"

In his office nearby, Jack Carter grinned across an antique oak desk. "You want to know about Betty?" he said. "Well, just about all I have to tell you is that I can't imagine what I'd do without her!"

Prestige? It's Wonderful . . . | *chapter* VII

The communications industries: advertising,
publishing, TV, and radio—The kind of girl
they recruit—Brains, talent, looks: does anyone
care?—The labor surplus in these fields: mini-
mum wages for maximum efficiency.

Just west of Fifth Avenue on 57th Street, around the corner
from Bergdorf Goodman and only a precious stone's throw
from Van Cleef & Arpels, there is an employment agency that
calls itself, with fine disregard for subtlety, Snob Jobs. It
caters not to the finished products of Chapin, Foxcroft, and
Miss Porter's School (though graduates of these schools are
prominent among its clientele), but, as its advertisements have
it, to "the discriminating taste." Simply put, Snob Jobs are
"specialists in advertising, public relations, television, and
allied fields."

The overwhelming appeal of the communications industries to the intelligent, career-minded young college woman is a phenomenon of the sixties, explicable, as Snob Jobs can testify, primarily in terms of prestige. An unmarried girl cannot be a status seeker on a two-car-garage level. Any kind of conspicuous consumption, in fact, is outside her reach and in all probability outside her interest. Time enough for the ranch house and the duplex; right now a three-room apartment and a presentable roommate will suffice. Wealthy people do not impress her; "gay," "creative," "amusing" ones do.

Now if each and every person who deserves or thinks he deserves those adjectives works in advertising, publishing, TV, *et al*, people outside the communications fields must be dull dogs indeed, and from the way communications-minded young women react when more prosaic employment is recommended, success consists of keeping outside the kennel. Thus the communications industries have become a snobocracy in themselves and have acquired, whether deservedly or not, a reputation as repositories of the creatively talented—the Harvards of the business world.

For the most part the girls who now want to go to Harvard are the same girls who have just left Vassar, which is to say that they have had a good liberal-arts education preparing them to go to work at nothing in particular. Thus everybody starts off on the same level of inexperience as everybody else, an advantage for the beginner that cannot be matched by fields requiring specialized training. Anyone who can read and write (but not type!), runs the theory, ought to be able to fill a niche somewhere in "communications."

There is a general tendency among graduates to lump the whole field together under the one title. The same glamorous aura that surrounds advertising hallows publishing; a job in television carries the same prestige as one in public relations.

While most girls do start out with a preference for one particular field they are just as happy to take a job in another, and there is constant changing of jobs from one field to the next. It is not until several years have passed that the specific job one does becomes important in terms of prestige; in the beginning, to be "in communications" is enough.

For a girl with feelings of inferiority, landing a job in the industry can be worth five years of psychoanalysis. It is a known fact that some firms, particularly certain of the large advertising agencies, select their trainees on what they delicately call an "all-round basis"—meaning appearance as well as intelligence. "From the moment I started work," says a now-married agency alumna, "I had a nice warm feeling of being not such a bad person, of maybe being even a little better than other people—of being wanted. All you had to do was look at the girls around you to see you were in pretty good company, and you figure, well, if *they* think I fit in here I guess I must be all right."

Firms like hers are necessarily highly competitive, both to get into and to advance in, and plenty of young women prefer to avoid the competition—which is tough enough even in places that *don't* want every prospective trainee to be a Miss America—and look elsewhere. Fortunately the industry is broad enough to absorb almost all of them, and it keeps on growing every year. A publishing house, for example, may set up a separate department on African affairs one year, on outer space the next. Advertising adds personnel in proportion to new accounts, which come in steadily as young organizations seek the prestige of being represented by old established agencies. Public-relations firms get bigger almost by the day, though in this field the smaller, newer firms have an unsettling habit of going out of business very suddenly.

Despite the constant expansion, the labor market in communications is no beginner's paradise. The same relatively nonexistent experience requirements that encourage one job hunter to apply also, naturally, attract every other, and the result is that every June a vast percentage of liberal-arts graduates floods the market. Many of them will not find jobs for months. This is because in the beginning most girls seek to identify themselves with the "name" firms, on the theory that it's good to be able to say one is "in advertising," but even better to say one is "with BBDO." Not until the giants of the industry have absorbed their yearly tribute is it the turn of the smaller firms, whose advantages (better pay, usually, for one) are set off by the disconcerting fact that a casual mention of their name is not enough to tell one's listener what one does.

Ironically, the girls who land the trainee jobs at the big firms are often the same girls who two or three years later shift over to the smaller ones, having discovered the unwritten law of communications averages: the larger the organization, the longer it will take to get ahead. It is rare to find a girl who had been out of college five years or more and is still working for the company she started out with. What happens to the girls who began in the smaller firms? Like water rushing in to fill a void, they go on to the larger ones, sacrificing immediate financial benefits for the excitement—and, of course, the prestige—of the giants.

Some young women who start out in communications stay on the job a much shorter time—a few months, perhaps; in some cases, only a few weeks. These are the girls who, talented and bright though they may be, lack—or disdain—the ability to keep up with the special kind of stress creative people create among themselves.

It would be interesting to compare the results of tests made on, say, an insurance company and a public-relations firm to determine the average level of blood pressure among the employees of each. How many insurance men die from heart attacks before fifty? How many PR men? Is there a significant difference? In the absence of such statistics we have only the general "image" of Madison Avenue, accepted by the public and attested to by people who ought to know, as a rat race. This term has become so familiar that it would probably turn up nine times out of ten on a word-association test ("Madison Avenue? Rat race"), and, usually happens when an idea is so generally taken for granted, apologists have begun to speak out on the other side, claiming that the image is false and that the industry is simply an innocent victim of misunderstanding.

Who's right? Everybody. Any business is bound to involve a certain amount of tension and intrigue. The point is that there does seem to be more of it in communications than anywhere else, just because the people who work on Madison Avenue are often the kind of people to begin with whose highly charged personalities have to be constantly involved with something besides business; who have to have some extra outlet for their emotions. What starts off as simple office routine—the promotion of a research assistant to writer, for example—becomes, as it recently did at a nationwide news magazine, a cause for grievance among those less lucky, and eventually involves most of the office personnel on one side or the other. In the process somebody is bound to get hurt, if for no other reason than that communications people, to a greater extent than others, cannot seem to leave their problems in the office but must bring them into their homes, their cocktail parties, their analysts' offices, so that every incident becomes new cause for soul searching. The conflicts are usually short-lived, but they are frequent, and highly emotional.

Whether the peculiar pressures of communications work (deadlines, strong inter-office competition as opposed to the "all-for-the-company" ideal, et cetera) put stress on the people, or whether the people really have the stress inside them to begin with, is a nice problem in cause and effect. There are good arguments on both sides. The case of the research worker cited above is an example of people reacting to outside pressures. An editor at a midtown publishing house tells a story of how people can come with the pressures built in.

"I hired a nice young kid as an assistant on the strength of an outstanding college record. There wasn't any doubt she had a good mind, but it appears she had a weird mechanical block. She was what they call a 'motor moron.' She couldn't for the life of her manipulate a typewriter or use a stapler or even a pencil sharpener. Believe me, we tried to teach her, but it was a hopeless case. She'd just get more and more exasperated and mad at herself and finally wind up in tears.

"After a few days I had to fire her, which by the way isn't easy. You never fire anybody that you don't suffer by it. But here's the odd part. This girl claimed she simply could not tell her parents she'd been fired. What the real reason was is anybody's guess, but she told me she couldn't tell her mother because her mother was 'breaking in a new maid.'

"The girl couldn't just be relocated; there was no place in the firm to put her. Since she couldn't tell her parents, she sat in our reception room—first she sat at her desk, till her replacement came—for two weeks, doing nothing from nine to five. She had to have someplace to go when she left home."

There are, of course, plenty of people who thrive on tension the way others do on vitamins, and it would seem that these are the ones most ideally suited to cope with Madison Avenue. Naturally there are rewards as well as headaches in communications. For men, these are primarily financial—on the higher levels the industry pays very well indeed—and, for women, prestigious. But both sexes concur in their appreciation of the "communications atmosphere"; the feeling, said one girl, that "you do meet marvelous, creative, stimulating people—" "Even if," added another, "80 per cent of them *are* in analysis."

It would seem logical that communications people are hired partly, at least, on the basis of talent, and this is almost invariably true of male personnel. Where women are concerned, however, general intelligence and appearance count for much more, to begin with, than creative potential. This is partly because women are not expected to work past the two or three years it takes them to find a husband, and too much talent in a beginner is rather more of a liability than an asset—making a girl dissatisfied, personnel managers claim, with a routine but necessary job. Another reason women are seldom hired for their talent is that most of the really creative jobs in the industry go, in the end, to men. Any truly talented woman can, with perseverance and patience, wind up with the kind of position she deserves, but on the way to the top she'll have a full-time job just to prove the creative ability that in a man would be taken for granted.

Like other business, communications has its share of "it's-not-what-you-know-but-who-you-know" personnel, who were hired on the strength of their "personal contacts." Actually there are probably more of these in the field than elsewhere, because aside from the president's sons, nieces, and cousins, they include a sizable group whose jobs depend upon their business connections—which, in fields such as publishing and public relations, are of vast importance. In these cases talent doesn't even come into the picture; if it's there, it's an extra dividend; if not, no one expected it anyway.

The only catch is that the who-you-know person's job is never absolutely secure unless he has so many contacts that the loss of one or two doesn't matter. An editor in a small publishing house tells of one woman who wasn't so lucky.

"She had been with the firm nearly thirty years," he recalls. "She was our one contact with a famous author—had met him in the thirties and brought him into the fold. All those years he wouldn't have any other editor but her. Then about two years ago he turned against her. He complained about her and said she wasn't getting him the resale rights he wanted. He didn't switch publishers, but he did switch editors, and all of a sudden she was out on her ear—fired, just like that. Fortunately for her, she had some stock in the company. She's now retired and spends most of her time traveling."

This total lack of job security is one of the major obstacles that people in communications must face. While most companies offer retirement plans, group medical insurance, and various other fringe benefits, there is no such thing as an industry-wide union of employees. Thus each firm dictates its own policy and sets its own wage scale, which usually weighs heavily in its own favor.

Starting salaries in advertising and public relations have over the past ten years remained consistently lower than in any other field. Today's advertising trainee can expect to make about 3500 dollars a year, on the average, as opposed to the 4000-dollar over-all average and the 5200 dollars offered chemists, mathematicians, and statisticians.

There are complaints, of course. But they are mostly good-humored complaints—the kind that are made because the complainers think it's expected of them. "We're violently underpaid—wage slaves!" "Serfs!" "Helpless captives in the toil of tyranny!"

"When it comes right down to it," summed up a TV girl Friday, "I'd ten times rather be right where I am with my piddling little 72-dollar salary, than making a great fortune in some deadly dull job and hating every minute of it I'm sure. And if you want proof that most everybody else thinks so too, just look at all the girls who'd like to get a job like mine."

Minimum wages for maximum efficiency? Most certainly— and the "wage slaves" love it.

... But Is It Worth It? | *chapter* VIII

Beginning "glamour" jobs—What they offer—
Sharpening pencils and liking it—The job
jumper versus the steady worker—Perseverance
does have some rewards.

There is a great deal to be said for a "glamour job," and often
a lot against it too.

"The secretaries and researchers here," said a young assistant editor of *Show* magazine, "are mostly very good-looking
rich girls who are willing to work hard for small salaries. They
all buy clothes at Bergdorf's and take home maybe 70 dollars
a week. They like the glamour of the job. It's a lot more fun,
if you're from Dayton, Ohio, and you went to Wellesley,
than working at an insurance firm."

"My mother and my friends think my job is real glamour,"
confided an administrative assistant at Barnes and Noble,
publishers of school textbooks. "My mother always pretends

I'm an editor. That's her idea of publishing; you're an editor or nothing. My married friends—all PTA types—think it's a big deal to know someone who works in textbooks."

"When I go to a fancy party for some visiting head of state, I sometimes forget that tomorrow morning I'll be cleaning up the library or calling fifty people for contributions," said an assistant at a non-profit foundation for foreign students. "Once a month or so, at dinners and receptions, my job takes on real glamour. The rest of the time it's pretty much mundane."

Mrs. C., an elderly supervisor in charge of trainees at an advertising agency, claimed that the girl who takes on the glamour job usually has two strikes against her to start. One, she expects the glamour to be readily apparent, and it isn't. Two, she hasn't given too much thought to what the job actually requires in the way of work, which is plenty. "It's hard enough," Mrs. C. said, "for a young person taking a full-time job for the first time simply to learn how to sit still. No more running out for coffee or a game of tennis like she did at college when she got bored with her studies. Add to that the fact that she must stick at the same thing all day long for seven or eight hours—very different from going from a class in sociology to a physics laboratory and then to a bridge game —and she begins to see that *any* job is a far cry from college work. 'Glamour' jobs in particular are often hard on young girls at first because, as I say, they seem to expect so much more than they get."

This situation, where it exists, isn't always the girl's fault.

"At the interview for my first job," said a Vassar graduate who began her career as "Girl Friday and general slave" in a small publishing house and is now an editor of children's books, "they seemed terribly interested in everything I'd done at college. They were vastly impressed, or acted like it, by my

having been editor of the lit mag, and class secretary. They
stressed the fact—I'm not imagining this, I remember it as
if it were yesterday because I've often thought of it afterward
—that my 'previous literary experience' would be taken into
consideration in whether I got the job, and that if I did it
would be a tremendous help in my work. Also that my 'well-
groomed appearance' would be a factor in my favor.

"After such a build-up could anyone blame me for thinking
the job must be something pretty special? I had vague visions
of myself, recommending an unsolicited manuscript and having it become a best seller—my 'previous literary experience,'
of course, enabling me to recognize a work of genius when
no one else gave it a second look—or suggesting revisions to
a famous author and having him say I'd inspired him to greater
heights. Such daydreams! But I thought, and still think, that
I was perfectly justified in having them, because I actually
hadn't been given the slightest inkling of what the job would
really be. I suppose they thought if I knew I'd be sharpening
pencils and getting coffee for people all day long I wouldn't
take the job, but they'd have been wrong. I wanted to work
in publishing, and I'd have accepted any job I was offered.
Only if I'd known what it involved at least there wouldn't have
been quite such a letdown. My 'well-groomed appearance'—
which I'd been half given to understand would be good in
meeting authors, agents, and people in the field—never got
me anything, unless you count being asked to a movie by
the mail boy.

"Once I recovered from the shock, and it really was that,
of finding that I didn't even have a desk of my own, and got
used to being called 'Mary' by people I had to call 'Mr. Brown'
and 'Miss Smith'—after that, it wasn't half bad. It took me,
I'd say, about two months to settle in, and while I can't say

I ever *enjoyed* the work, I did eventually come to like it. Once you make up your mind that you yourself are no big deal and aren't likely to be for a long while yet, you start to appreciate the people around you who *are;* also those who will be and some who won't. In most any job it's the people who matter, and the glamour jobs do have the exciting people. In the end, that first job, the people in the office, gave me more of an education than I ever got in college courses in psychology."

Not every disillusioned beginner becomes a happy, seasoned employee, of course. Some girls leave before the benefits of the job have become apparent; others stay put, hating every minute of it but not knowing what else to do. Sometimes what begins as a pleasant job becomes a difficult one if the process of analysis—which starts when a girl has learned enough about her job to begin thinking in terms of how *it* works, rather then how *she* does—sets in.

A non-profit foundation worker, a Phi Beta Kappa graduate of Barnard, illustrates the point. Interviewed after she had been on the job six months, she had this to say:

"On balance, I am happy with my job. The salary is good. The job came along when I needed it. I have a lot of freedom. It is not bureaucratized. I don't feel over- or underworked, and I think I'm doing an effective job. I hope it will involve more creativity in the future."

After another year she was again interviewed and asked what, if anything, had happened to make her dissatisfied with her work.

"Non-profit organizations," she began, "have a neurotic psychology. They have people with their hearts in the right place; people who are concerned with mankind. But many of the people are there for their own neurotic reasons: personal dissatisfaction; an inability to cope with the people they must relate to on a more personal level. And they therefore take on humanity. That's much easier for them.

"There are many single people in these organizations. They take on the organization as their whole life. They don't work from nine to five, but from nine to seven, and are continually worried about it. Every office crisis takes on a personal meaning. There's total involvement; everyone hates or loves everyone else a great deal. So there's so much office politics—which I hate.

"They tend to think their own projects are all-important and run down everyone else's. This sometimes makes me think I am working for a rival organization from everyone else's in the office.

"These people have a need to say, 'Oh, I had to stay in the office till seven last night,' and to say how busy they are, which as far as I can see only says how lonely and embittered they are. Single women get terrible loyalties, to the big boss, or to their particular boss. He becomes the boss in all of her life. And she doesn't let anyone else get near him.

"Another problem with organizations like mine is that everyone is a thinker. No one wants to do the work. The projects of the moment get done, but the long-range things get neglected. Actually I have come to the conclusion that the job I now have isn't a useful job, in the sense of what I am doing. I think that both the organization and I could be done very well without. However, I'll give it another year or so. There are certain satisfactions that I might begin to find. It does hold certain challenges. All in all, though, I look forward to leaving."

Her analysis of her organization may be more cynical than correct, and maybe not. Cynicism, unfortunately, is easier to come by than good judgment, especially in the glamour jobs. Take Vida Grayson, twenty-three-year-old publicist who is nursing a second ulcer. Her cynicism takes the form of a daily two-martini lunch, despite strict doctor's orders to drink little else but milk. "I could cut out the martinis, of course," she says, "but then I'd have no defense against the strain at work, which is how I got sick in the first place. Every day I'm trying to do things on different levels, constantly suppressing what I really feel. You have to be nice to everyone . . . it's not easy for me. I might as well enjoy the cocktail, because I'm going to have ulcers whether I do or not."

Or Barbara Blitstein, who for seven years has been helping to produce documentary television films. "I've often thought of leaving my job. You take it out on your friends and talk about leaving and then feel, well, it's all baby stuff, like smoker talk. I guess in any company there are hard periods of time. Three years after I came, the head of the department—my father image—was fired. They said the demands of the job were getting too much for him. I was all shaken up. I couldn't understand why people who'd worked for him a long time didn't protest. Looking back, of course, I can see it was because they were shown that the firing was to their advantage. They got increases, for example. Maybe they were bought off. Even I made out all right. My supervisor was shoved upstairs and I got her job."

On the higher levels of the glamour industries the "demands of the job" are usually quoted to explain everything, from ulcers to firing to expense-account paddings. "Most of the things I do," stated a TV newscaster, "are O.K. because they're in the line of work. Expense-account padding—well, it's very minor. There are even times I think I've lost. I don't pad more than 7 dollars a week. I once put in a 7.50 expense account for three weeks, at the beginning of my job. It was handed back to me. Everyone in the office pads expense accounts, including your bosses. It's a known thing, so I don't feel morally wrong about it. When I first came here I was far more concerned about it than I am now. You forget about it after a while. You don't weigh the moral questions every time you put in an account."

Despite the headaches, moral and otherwise, the percentage of young women who, having once held a glamour job, transfer to work outside communications is apparently quite low. Job jumpers are common but they jump within the field and usually for reasons of better pay or more prestige rather than dissatisfaction with the previous job. There are always exceptions, of course, such as the government girl who gave up a job "with a good salary and great status" for one with less of each because "the scope of my former job was reduced and I simply got bored." (Unable to quit, which would have jeopardized her government career, she had to arrange to be fired, and was, on grounds of reduction of staff, with 1000 dollars' severance.)

Unlike other industries, there is no stigma attached to changing jobs in communications; if anything, the opposite is true. The correct reaction to "I've got a new job" would be, "Good for you," rather than, "What went wrong where you were?" It is taken for granted that any new job must be better than an old one.

Thus any girl who stays in the industry long enough, whether the entire time be spent with the same firm or whether she changes jobs every two or three years, is almost certain to wind up in a high-salary, high-status position, and that goes even for the girl of only mediocre ability. If talent doesn't get her to the top you can bet that someday seniority —meaning sheer, dogged refusal-to-get-married-and-quit-work stick-to-it-iveness—will.

Five-o'clock Shadow | *chapter IX*

After office hours: what kind of lives career girls lead—Family status—Do they support others?— Save any money?—Boy friends: who they date, where they go, how they handle men.

When five o'clock comes and the office staff goes, the career girl is on her own again. All day long her time belongs to other people; now it's hers to spend or waste any way she wants.

What she does during the day may or may not determine her evening.

If she's in publishing, assuming her job is fairly important (meaning almost anything with a "title") or she knows someone else whose is, there's usually a party being given for or by some literary personality a few nights a week. All she's got to do is get invited to one; from there on she's got it made because everybody will be talking about the next and they'll simply assume she'll be there. This is known as "getting on the circuit."

If she's in advertising there will be occasional "presentation" parties at which a new client meets the staff or a new sales campaign is introduced, but these are more often given during the day and don't approach the scale of the book blasts. Ad agencies do not give a girl many chances to meet people from other ad agencies. The competition is too intense for socializing.

If she works for a news magazine, other people's leisure hours are her most frantic. Ten P.M. of a Sunday night may find her wildly pasting, cutting, or proofreading a story that broke five hours ago and has to make the magazine in time for the Monday-morning mailing.

If she's in TV, movies, public relations, or newspaper work there's always a free movie somewhere in town. Major studios send out thousands of invitations to private film showings, and the man sitting next to her is just as likely to be Joe Doakes of the mailroom as Howard Taubman of the *Times*. Getting hold of these invitations is fairly easy: a girl simply finds out which department in her firm they're addressed to and gets friendly with the people there. An invitation allows the recipient to bring along one other person; why shouldn't she be the one? The girl who is really in, of course, is the one whose name is on the envelope.

Then there are art-gallery openings, private concerts, previews of plays, and museum exhibitions, all of which come complete with glittering cocktail parties. Finding out about and getting invited to every "event" in New York City is well-nigh impossible (though Broadway columnists do a good job of it), but if a girl is interested enough to work at it she can usually count on at least one party a night. If all goes well the party will produce an invitation to dinner and, if it's really her night, to another party.

Ninety per cent of these star-studded wingdings do not require any tickets or identification, except in the case of movie and theater previews. The people who give them and the people who go to them seem to assume automatically that anybody who knows about the party belongs there, and in any case there are enough drinks and hors d'oeuvres to feed three times as many as come.

It is not true to say that any girl who wants this kind of night life can have it. If she doesn't happen to work in communications, getting started on the circuit is hard. She'll have to depend entirely on people who do to tell her where the action is, and if she doesn't know anyone outside the paper-bag company it may be impossible.

To the girl on the outside looking in, New York's party people may seem pretty glamorous creatures. But if it's any comfort to her, plenty of young women who have made the scene, and seen it all, opt out. New York can turn a girl awfully blasé if it gives her too much of a good thing.

"It's nothing to me to be taken anywhere in this town any more. I'd rather spend an evening cooking a guy a steak in my apartment than go to a first night—having had enough of first nights. Nothing's a production any more. I'm absolutely unimpressionable."

Better to have been bored than never to have been at all? Maybe—and maybe not.

Actually, what a girl does after five depends more on who she is and what she's like than on where she works, which is why it's never possible to predict exactly how Miss X in the ad agency will spend the evening. There are thousands of Miss Xs, every one of them with her own background, upbringing, prejudices, and preferences, and it would be a sad state of affairs if all were to react alike in every situation. The girl who was the class grind at college isn't likely to metamorphose into the office flirt just because there are three men in her firm to every woman. More likely she'll be found spending as many of her evenings with books as with boys; she prefers it that way and always has. Similarly, the extrovert who shines in a crowd won't become a hermit because she's the only one in her office under sixty; she'll find some way of going where the crowd goes.

To some extent a girl's social life in New York City or any other large city depends upon her family status. If she's sending home half her weekly paycheck, there's not much left after rent and food bills are paid for anything else, and this can and does affect her leisure time. One girl said she preferred to date men who took her for a walk in the park rather than to dinner at an expensive restaurant, simply because she couldn't afford the kind of clothes big-city night life demands.

A study of young working women made some years ago in Chicago turned up four distinct patterns of home and family relationship among girls whose salaries help support their families. These are:

1. The girl who is autocratically dominated by her parents, without regard to her wishes, interests, or ambitions. Parental control may center about handling money.
2. The girl who contributes financially to family unity, has never imagined herself outside the family, and finds most of her interests satisfied by it.
3. The girl who accepts financial responsibility and is loyal to her parents, but carries on other phases of life in accordance with her own wishes.
4. The girl who is the "man of the house"—usually the only child of a widowed mother. Daughter earns all the money to support them both.

To these, add the girl who neither gives money to her family nor receives it, and the girl whose family supports her entirely, and you have just about the whole picture. The latter category, at least among girls who live away from home, is negligible.

Among college graduates, a majority is self-supporting and sends no money home. When they do, however, it is often a great deal of money, in contrast to non-college graduates, most of whom *do* help at home but seldom contribute more than 25 per cent of their salaries to the family. Those B.A.s who help their parents financially are, nine times out of ten, young women who won scholarships to college.

The smaller the paycheck, the more likely it is to be split two ways. The reason is clear: girls in routine jobs that pay little—file clerks, bookkeepers, receptionists, typists, et cetera—are seldom college girls. Simply by knowing what her job is and/or if she went to college (except for the scholarship winners), it is often possible to predict whether a girl helps support her family.

When it comes to saving and spending money, the college-non-college rule of thumb is again a good indicator. Self-supporting college women make more to start with, yet their savings are out of all proportion to their earnings when matched against those of non-college graduates. If Betty Coed makes 90 dollars a week, she'll save from 20 to 30 dollars, or nearly a third of her take-home pay. Tillie the Toiler, on the other hand, makes about 70 dollars a week, contributes 10 to 20 dollars to her family, and saves an average of 5 dollars, or only one-tenth of what's left. If the money Tillie sent home were counted as savings, she'd be putting away as much as Betty does—only it won't work that way because Tillie wouldn't do it. Queried as to what they'd do with the extra 20 dollars if they weren't forced to contribute it to family finances, 13 out of 16 non-college graduates picked at random replied, "Spend it" (on clothing, entertainment, and travel, in that order).

One Cornell graduate came up with a theory in reverse about saving money. "When you have no money," she said, "relative amounts are meaningless. I bought 175 dollars' worth of Christmas presents my first year in New York, and spent the rest of the year paying off the bills. But when you earn 95 dollars a week money becomes important and you pinch pennies."

This kind of spending can drive parents crazy, particularly when the family could use some extra money. Here is an excerpt from a letter written by one harassed mother.

> Let me tell you a little of the live-at-home we have in our house and you'll soon see my peeve. My daughter is twenty. She has a job that pays $63 a week before taxes. She doesn't give one cent toward household expenses, which are quite large (we own a mortgaged house). My husband is a $5600-a-year man. I work two days a week to help with expenses. When I ask my daughter to help she says she can't afford to and we don't need it. I tried to explain to her we shouldn't have to need it and her money might ease the situation a little. Also I tried to point out to her for her own self-respect she should want to help, but there's no talking to her.

Almost every day she comes home with packages. *Shoes*, bags, gloves, *shoes*, dresses, album records galore, *shoes*, lipsticks by the dozen, sweaters she couldn't wear out in a lifetime, slacks any and everytime she sees a pair she likes. I try to tell her to buy less and she diets every so often and needs a new size afterward. Then either she has to have them tailored or discarded but there's no stopping her. This is a girl who can't afford to give a nickel for her comforts and upkeep in the home she lives in. She cleans her room once a week but that's all. If she has a glass of water she leaves the glass in the sink for someone else to wash.

Please don't say the usual, "Well, you spoiled her." It's not true. When she went to school she was well dressed but not extravagantly so. She *didn't* get everything she wanted.

For the first month or two my daughter did give $10 a week at home. Then suddenly she decided she wouldn't.

The major difference between Betty Coed's savings and Tillie the Toiler's is that the former saves as a matter of principle and the latter for the things money can buy. Once a college girl starts building up a savings account, she is reluctant to touch it, unless it be to invest the money in stocks or bonds. She'll tell you she's saving "for the future" or because "you never know when you'll need capital" or simply because "having a few hundred dollars saved up makes a girl feel more independent." The average non-graduate, on the other hand, saves money for an immediate purpose. Either she's got her eye on that new spring suit in Best's window, or she and a friend are vacationing in the mountains next summer. Her savings account seldom has any entries in the "interest" column because before the three months are up she's withdrawn the entire principal.

Family status and means of support may, in really extreme cases, affect a girl's entire out-of-the-office life, especially if she happens to fall into category number four of the Chicago study: "only daughter of a widowed mother."

"I live at home for financial reasons," said a Vassar '59 alumna who is her mother's main support. "I'm not at all happy there; the apartment is very small, I don't have my own room, and I don't like crowded quarters with someone very much my senior. Our relationship isn't particularly congenial even under the best of circumstances."

Constant tension at home began making this girl "nervous at work and tense with boys." She finally sought the help of a psychoanalyst, thus worsening her situation by putting the stamp of permanency on it ("It would be impossible for me to maintain two households at this time, including my psychiatric care").

From a "normal" social life ("two or three dates a week"), she has "withdrawn from the world . . . because I have been seeing an analyst." Her difficulties with her mother ("whom I resent because she's such a drain on my finances, and my resentment of course comes through to her and there's not much I can do about it") seem to have extended to men, so that she pulls back from anything resembling a "normal" relationship.

"My amount of dating, in the sense of real dating, has been minimal in the last year. I have several men friends in the theater world who are homosexuals. I often go to their homes for dinner. This is a far easier kind of relationship for me than the regular dating. No pressure, none of the unsaid things in a romantic relationship. They have different tastes from other men. They have made their own homes. They are excellent hosts and good cooks.

"I like these people as people. In case you're wondering, they look like men. I wouldn't like men who flutter around and look like fags."

Another girl, five years out of Russell Sage College and accustomed to living away from home, recently lost her father and is now planning to return. She is resigned to the situation, but instinct and observation have her worried.

"I rather doubt I will be happy living alone with my mother, but it's out of practical necessity and I have to give it a shot. I foresee mother conflict. I don't know anyone who doesn't have it."

Other girls who live alone with their mothers agree that the situation affects their social lives to a greater or lesser extent.

"I was dating an Algerian boy and my mother objected. She kept saying, 'How will it look to the neighbors?' I had to meet him downstairs. Pretty soon he stopped asking me out."

"My mother wonders how I can enjoy just taking a walk someplace with a guy. I don't bother telling her what I do any more. I learned later than most people not to tell all."

Not every daughter of a widowed mother has these problems; only those who are where they are because they *have* to be. When there's enough money in the family to give a girl a choice, as often as not she'll decide to stay put.

"I have my own floor in our apartment. I come and go as I please. I like it where I am. I suppose that if my mother ever pressured me about getting married, say, or if I ever fell in love with someone she didn't approve of, I'd move out. But not now, certainly. The boys I know say I'd be out of my mind. Why stamp yourself as a career girl in the rat race? they say. The girls, though, all tell me to leave. Like rats in a sinking ship, they want to pull me with them."

Among young women who are self-supporting and live alone or with other girls, this attitude is considered "immature" and a real liability where men are concerned.

"I believe," said one, "that living at home hinders getting

married. You're too comfortable, too protected. This way, you know what you're capable of as an individual and as a woman. You get the feeling you can do for yourself, and then when you know *that* you know the next step is to do it for someone else."

Perfectly true, said her date, and "what's more," he added, "independence comes *only* from living on your own. A woman stays a child even if she's thirty-five if she's living with her family."

Girls who live alone sincerely feel that they have a head start on the stay-at-homes in the dating market. Faced with a choice, they say, a man prefers an informal atmosphere. He'd rather converse with a girl's roommate while he's waiting for her to get dressed for a date than with her parents, they claim.

Not surprisingly, those who live alone or with other girls seem to date more than those who live at home; an average of four times a week as compared to twice. This is because they make a great many more "casual" dates of the "why-don't - you - stop - up - for - a - drink - at - my - place - to - night?" variety, which lead, as often as not, to dinner, either at her apartment or in a restaurant.

"The men I date," said a twenty-four-year-old magazine assistant, "seem to like staying around the apartment and having dinner. I've made at least ten dinners for dates in the last two months. I have it down to a system now, a standard dinner: salad, steak; in summer, wine. You really can't ruin steak. If he's cosmopolitan, I serve snails and Scotch before dinner and Cointreau after."

Girls who live at home shy away from this kind of informal girl-asks-man variety of dating. ("I don't have my own kitchen, so how can I ask a man up for dinner? Anyway, if

I did, and my parents were there, he'd think I was trying to snag him; and if they *weren't* there he'd wonder why not. It's too complicated all around.") As a consequence they date less during the week and at least as much or more on weekends. To make up for not having them to dinner, they usually ask their dates in for a drink or coffee after the Saturday-night movie.

Dinner and movies is far and away the most common way of spending a night out in New York, especially if a couple is on a blind date. "Over a dinner table," said one girl, "you can get to know a person pretty well. Then if it's obvious to both of you that you weren't exactly made for each other, a movie is the best way to avoid having to make conversation for the rest of the evening. If you do feel like talking more, or if you're with someone you really like and want to spend more time with, you can always go for a drive, or a walk in the park."

For a memorable evening out, most young women would choose the theater, preferably preceded by dinner and followed by dancing. The average girl, unless she happens to be in the business, considers herself lucky if she's taken to a show once every two months. Some, of course, never see any plays at all and others turn up regularly at every first night. It depends partly on the field a girl works in (girls in the communications industries seem to score the highest on the "how-many-of-these-plays-have-you-seen?" checklists) and partly on the man she dates.

"I don't seem to be able to attract the kind of guys who take you to plays," said a research analyst rather wistfully. "My dates mostly take me out to beer joints."

It may be hard at first, girls say, just *getting* a date in New York. Roommates are some help ("We introduce our dates to each other and often double date") but large parties seem to be the quickest and most dependable way of meeting men.

"The party is definitely best," asserted an Oberlin graduate who shares a large apartment with two other girls. "We've given about one a month ourselves. My roommate works at A.B.C. and knows literally five hundred people; sometimes it seems like half of them are in our place at once. Then, of course, they invite you back to theirs."

Parties are fine, agreed another girl, just so long as they keep coming in a steady stream. When there are long stretches in between, she said, her social life suffers. "When I came here in September I knew absolutely no one. I didn't go to my first party till December. I met maybe five or six guys there and went out till February with guys from that party."

Then, she said, the phone stopped ringing.

"I think guys here run in cycles. They take you out three or four times and then if they think nothing's going to come of it they stop. So in February I knew no one again.

"Oh, there are the men at work, but going out with them is almost more trouble than it's worth, if you know what I mean."

What she meant would be understood instantly by almost any working girl. Wherever possible, girls prefer to date men who do not work in the same place they do.

One petite young typist at a Wall Street law firm who is surrounded all day by eligible future partners (both legal and matrimonial) put it this way. "I don't like to go out with people in the firm. If you say boo to anybody here, everyone thinks you're engaged."

A twenty-three-year-old editorial assistant in a publishing

house admitted, with some reluctance, that she was dating a co-worker.

"Normally," she said, "I don't advocate office romances. It happens that other people in the office don't know about mine. My boy friend thinks it might endanger his position [he is an editor] if people talked—and they would. Mostly, it's none of anyone's business. But in my office we're so close we know all each other's private lives—so it's hard."

Co-worker or chance acquaintance, a man is a man is a man. "Every unmarried woman has a constant battle with men," argued a panel of lady authors on a recent radio program, "either to defend her virtue or to get a husband."

Unfortunately, those who succeed in the "either" sometimes lose out on the "or." Still, as far as the average girl is concerned, there oughtn't to be any distinction. If he's the guy who means to do her right—he'll wait.

Marriage . . . Maybe | *chapter* X

*Problems of the single girl over twenty-five—
She may not want to marry—Why—How her
job affects her decision—Divorce rate is a factor.*

A man without a woman
Is like a raft upon the sand,
But if there's one thing worse in this universe,
It's a woman without a man.

They used to sing it at football games and fraternity parties,
and they believed it with all their hearts. They sing it still,
occasionally, at Joe King's German Rathskeller, or Michael's
Pub, or P. J. Clarke's, but the old fervor is gone and in its
place is a shade of resentment. Nowadays it cuts a little too
close to the bone.

"They" are the over-twenty-fives, for whom marriage,
which a very few years ago was something-that-would-be, is
every day coming nearer to something-that-should-have-been.

Somewhere between the ages of twenty and twenty-five, almost without their noticing it, nearly all their friends, acquaintances, classmates got married. And after a while the wedding invitations ceased and the birth announcements started coming in.

When did they stop being "recent college graduates," "girls," "the group," and become, socially and statistically, "single women?" For some, it happened the day their best friend married; for others, the day of their twenty-fifth birthday. Being single is certainly a fact of life, but, like being married, it is also a state of mind.

"I never think of myself as single. I think of myself as not yet married."

"I'm horribly conscious of being twenty-six and still single."

"I can remember thinking anyone who wasn't married by twenty-five was an old maid. Now I think you're not an old maid till you're past forty."

"I'm twenty-eight and I don't happen to have a husband yet. So what?"

It is probably true to say that no girl thinks of herself as "single" unless and until she wants to be married. One New Year's Eve she makes a private resolution: "*This* year I'm going to get married." If it doesn't happen that way, doubt sets in. "Before, I didn't want to get married and I wasn't. Now I do, but I'm still not. Am I going to be an old maid? What's wrong with me?"

Caught between their "Why-aren't-you-married?" friends and their "get-married-but-only-to-the-right-man" parents, some girls take whatever's available at the moment they decide they're ready for a husband. One unmarried twenty-six-year-old at a large firm claims to have seen several such.

"It's a vicious circle. They decide they want to quit working and get back to the suburbs. But they really don't know *what* they want; only what they're supposed to have. I don't think they ever meet the 'right' man; they find a presentable guy and con themselves into thinking they're mad about him. They're not happy, they're frantic."

Not altogether true, says another single girl in the same firm.

"The cynics automatically assume that anybody over twenty-five who happens to find a husband is using marriage as an escape valve. It seems to me you have to have a pretty low opinion of your fellow woman if you can think that way. After all, a girl who's been to college and been out in the world a few years ought to be given credit for *some* intelligence. I can't believe that a girl could go into marriage, with her eyes wide open, knowing all the time she doesn't love the guy and just thinking somehow she'll make a go of it. I suppose some people do, but there can't be many."

The girl who decides she wants to get married and does, is often the girl who can't understand what's taking somebody else so long. "Anyone who really wants a husband can have one. What's she waiting for, Santa Claus?"

"Anybody who really wants a husband can have one"—unthinking words that are absolutely sure to bring the singles out fighting.

"I disagree strongly with the theory that if you want to get married you will. Thank God my parents have never said that! I believe that circumstance—just sheer luck—plays the most important role in whether you are or are not married. I think I know myself well enough to know that I really do want to marry, and not a knight on a white charger either. So far I just haven't been lucky."

"I do *not* believe that 'anyone who wants to get married

can.' It's not a matter of luck, either. It's a matter of neurotic problems, for the one who isn't married and wants to be, like me. I feel that if I don't get married I will never function to my fullest capacity. The girl who is not married, and doesn't want to be, and says so, at least copes successfully with *one* end of it!"

"It's not true that a girl can get married whenever she wants to. People who say that are the same ones who say you don't have to be in love when you marry; that the relationship grows and love comes later. I think that's abominable. I'd respect someone's mistress more than someone who marries without being in love."

The single girl who wants to get married, but only to the "right" man, may find herself going around in circles. If she's unhappy, is it because she's single or because she isn't married? There's a difference.

"I'll get married because I want to, not because I have to— though I *do* have to, I guess, because I'll be unhappy unless I do."

Some are philosophical.

"I don't think marriage is a panacea. I mean this: you *have* to start somewhere. You *have* to believe that marriage was the way it was all meant to be. I think part of the need of every man and woman is to be mated and reproduce, and there is frustration if you can't do this. Given the mores of our society, marriage is the way to do this."

Others are worried.

"I'm pretty sure I'll get married sometime, except for my many low moments. My job makes up for a lot, but not for everything. It couldn't. To me, the happiest state would be to be happily married and be able to work at the same time. The worst thing, I think, would be to have a bad marriage."

Still others are downright scared.

"I'm afraid I'll get so desperate I'll marry the wrong guy. I'm very afraid that none of the things I want will be fulfilled."

If you ask a single girl over twenty-five what she wants most in the world the answer, in one form or another, is "happiness." Most of them go on to equate happiness with love and marriage—but not all. There are a surprising number of young women today for whom marriage has picked up a good many minuses—so many, in fact, that the balance is no longer automatically on the credit side.

The reservations seem to mount in proportion to age. Very few girls just out of college ever consider the possibility that they might not marry in the near future. But by the time they're twenty-five the picture changes. Secure in their jobs, settled in their apartments, safe in their daily routines, these are the career girls who, if not exactly avoiding the altar, are not stampeding toward it either.

They've accumulated a lot of dust under their feet since school days, and they're no longer sure they want it—and themselves—swept away.

"I've got a good job, enough money for what I need, and independence. Nobody tells me where to go or what to do. Why tie myself down to a husband and a house full of screaming kids?"

Sour grapes?

Not always. In fact, not too often. Oh, there are the man haters, and the professional spinsters, and those who've tried and failed and never tried again, and the embittered few who would have married anyone but were never asked. But thousands of unmarried working girls twenty-five and up (an arbitrary line, actually; no one can say for sure when the romantic dies and the realist is born) live alone and love it.

Of all the reasons for this widespread state of single bless-edness (and they run the gamut from socio- to psycho- to il-logical), two stand out: money and divorce.

The older a girl gets, the more her working skills improve, and the higher the price she commands in the labor market. A typist becomes an executive secretary; a researcher, an editor; a trainee, a copywriter. By the time she's twenty-seven, with five to nine years of experience behind her, the average secretary is earning at least 100 dollars a week and in many cases up to 130 dollars. Girls who stick it out in publishing can expect about the same; advertising, public relations, and television go even higher, with 250 dollars a week a not-un-common salary for a TV newswriter or an experienced fash-ion copywriter.

This is where the money-versus-marriage angle comes in. A girl at twenty-seven is at the peak of her earning power; unless she becomes one of the city's few top women executives she'll never make much more than she is now. But a man—that is, a man in her own age group—has hardly begun. If he's a doctor, he's barely out of medical school; if a lawyer, work-ing for someone else's firm or just getting started in his own; if an accountant, engineer, teacher, or businessman, still only earning about a third of what he can someday expect. The young men in her own field make about as much or a little more than she does, and you can't start raising a family on *that*—not, at least, in the style to which she has become ac-customed.

So she has three possibilities. One: marry a young man and manage as best they can, living adequately but never quite comfortably. Two: find an older man, usually one in his for-ties. A rare breed. Most of them are already taken, though sometimes they don't admit it till there's no other way out. Three: stay single.

Cold statistics, which seldom if ever get down to warm cases, say that the unmarried twenty-five-year-old has only one chance in four of becoming a wife. What the record fails to show, and what most people—men, in particular—fail to recognize, is that she may be single because she wants it that way. "Only God will help the working girl," they say. "God helps those who help themselves," she retorts.

"When I was fresh out of college and making 60 dollars a week I thought if I didn't get married soon I'd probably starve to death. Peanut-butter-and-marshmallow sandwiches—how I loathed them!"

Salvation—and an occasional steak—came to this girl not in the shape of Prince Charming but in the form of a job promotion. With an extra 20 dollars in her weekly paycheck marriage no longer seemed an immediate necessity. She began to eat better, dress better, and wait until "the right man—not just some guy who happened to have a little money—" came along.

So it went. Somewhere along the line the outer limits of the waiting period grew hazy. Another promotion, another raise, a new apartment, and the transformation from impoverished-and-man-hunting-graduate to self-sufficient-and-selective-businesswoman was complete.

"I'm so different now. I have self-confidence. I matured a lot in five years. It's partly having made the 'status jump.' I think that's crucial—if not to your value system, at least to your psychological system. I feel I really live here. I have my bank account here and my income-tax returns come here. I like it. I can afford to wait now."

"Having some money of my own has made me a better prospect for a wife, I think. I used to think, 'The man I marry will have money.' Now I think, 'The man I marry, if he has money, will have made it himself.' He'll have a sense that life is for enjoying, and is fulfilling and meaningful; that you have the capacity to make what you do in life. I hate tight people—it doesn't matter how much money they have. I hate constipated people."

Balancing the "good" of having one's own money (nice clothes, good apartment, more freedom, et cetera) against the "bad" (it scares men away, makes a girl "tough" and "hard"), many over-twenty-fives come down on the side of the dollar. They wouldn't do it over again—i.e., marry young—if they could, they say. Not surprisingly there is strong disagreement on this point from concerned parents.

"I worry terribly about Marcia, to tell you the truth," said one mother. "I'm not sure what she's trying to prove. She's a great business success, we all know that. She's always been competitive; at camp, in college, at work, and she's usually gotten what she wanted. She seems to think everything's a challenge in life. I've been waiting for her to realize marriage is a challenge too, but she says, 'Oh, Mother, anyone can get married, I'll wait till I'm good and ready.' If you ask me, she's got more money than is good for her. It makes a girl too independent. They start thinking they don't need anybody else. I never wanted Marcia to marry too young, but now I'm afraid she'll never get married at all. The trouble with these girls is they have such a good time they don't think about the future, and then one day they wake up and it's too late."

Divorce, the second factor that keeps the working girl in the office and out of the home, also looms larger the older she gets. "Ve get too soon old and too late schmart," said the Pennsylvania Dutch philosopher, but the unmarried twenty-six-year-old, though young in years, is old indeed in wisdom.

She has, to put it mildly, seen too much too soon. Most if not all of her high-school and college friends have married, and not a one of them but seems to think that Susie Single's shoulder was created especially for her to cry on. In-law problems, straying husbands, sibling rivalry—you name it, Susie's heard it.

Her own troubles, of course, are minor compared to those of her married friends—or so they seem to think. After all, they say, an unfriendly co-worker or a boss with more than business on his mind can be easily disposed of: "If I were you I'd quit!" (She's only worked there eight years. Seniority? What's that?)

Divorce, on the other hand, is something everyone has heard of. Startling as it may seem, the Census Bureau says that one out of every four marriages in America is doomed from the word go. And to listen to some of the single girls in New York City, you'd think that every one of the future divorcées lived right there.

"I am happier now than I have been at any other time," said Barbara Carll, twenty-six. "The more I see of my friends' lives, the more I like my own. Most of the marriages I see around me are pretty awful. If it's not one thing it's another. Come to think of it, among the people I know, the majority are divorced or remarried."

Barbara, a junior executive in a Fifth Avenue department store, is not the cynical type. Her wide gray eyes are sincere and reflect an active and sympathetic interest in people—a pleasant personal attribute that also happens to be essential to her job.

Unlike the great majority of working girls, Barbara does not

support herself. Her parents pay the rent, gas, electricity, and
telephone bills for her three-room apartment on East 68th
Street. She spends her 90-dollar salary on food, clothes, entertainment, and a twice-a-week maid, and usually saves about
30 dollars a month.

Most of Barbara's divorced friends envy her. She suspects
that many of the married ones do too.

"I've seen the way they look when they come up here. Sort
of—it's hard to explain—weary. One friend of mine with three
kids under five comes up every other Saturday afternoon like
clockwork. She once told me it was her 'rest cure.' I ask myself, 'Can it be my imagination or are they really as tired of
life as they look?' My own life is still just beginning. Theirs
seems to be all over, yet we're the same age. Well, if and when
I *do* get married, at least I'll know what I'm in for."

It is precisely Barbara's kind of obviously well-ordered exist-
ence, quiet and comfortable and free from surface tension,
that seems to bring out the worst in the discontented wife.
Girls like Barbara can and do expect to be bombarded with
other people's problems. They're Everywoman's mother, sis-
ter, psychoanalyst, from their closest friends to the dimly remembered classmates they meet on the subway. Yet all the
complainers, without exception, raise their eyebrows and
wonder if there's not something wrong with the poor girl
when she says, "I am definitely not sorry I haven't gotten
married."

The real tragedy is that the marrieds never, never tell the
singles about the happy times—the moments of shared ten-
derness and mutual feeling—that, in the end, so far outnum-
ber the petty disputes. For one thing, they prefer, quite understandably, to hug such moments to themselves. For another,
they don't want to make life any harder than it already is for

the girl alone by seeming to gloat over their own good fortune.

When trouble comes, wives look for sympathy. When all is well, their single friends never know about it. The distorted picture of wifehood that emerges from the talks—and the silences—can very well discourage an impressionable young woman from thoughts of marriage.

Fortunately for society, though, today's career girls are no dopes. The majority of young women, despite the things they see, hear, and read about marriage, have the sense to sort out good from bad; to say to themselves, "After all, if it were as awful as some of my friends make it sound, nobody would *ever* get married!" Their real task is to maintain objectivity in the face of a one-sided barrage; to realize that, if married life as lived by a few of the people they know seems a not-so-flowery path of problems, they may be missing the roses for the thorns.

All Work and No Play | chapter XI

The weekend whirl—Saturday and shopping habits—Where and what they buy—The kind of clothes they feel they must wear—Sunday: from solitary crossword puzzlers to compulsive party givers—Vacations: where they go and why.

Working girls start weekends late. Of all the things people can do in a big city in their leisure time, they have three standout favorites, and sleeping is one of them. Talk to any group of ten girls and nine of them will tell you they never get up before ten on Saturday and often sleep till noon Sundays.

Some psychiatrists say that oversleeping, or unneeded sleep, may be a way of rejecting life. According to one analyst, the woman just out of college and experiencing her first contact with the adult business world is at a crossroads: if she hasn't completely matured, and not many have, she's expected to do so now, all at once, fast. The pressure brought on by a new job, new apartment, new people; the responsibilities of being self-supporting and having to make one's own decisions without parental advice, may easily, he says, cause inner conflicts that cannot be resolved in any simple way. Sleep thus becomes both an escape from one's problems and a subconscious protest against having to grow up and go to work.

Many girls are quick to admit that there is some truth in this theory where they themselves are concerned, but they don't give it much thought. "After all," said one, "if I sleep late because I have problems, and then start worrying about oversleeping, I'll just have more problems, won't I?"

Some sleepers have positive reasons of their own for staying in bed.

"This is the first time in four years that I've been able to sleep as late as I wanted on weekends. In college you had to get up early or you'd miss breakfast, and anyway the noise in the halls woke you. I'm just making up for lost time."

"I figure this is my last chance to sleep as late as I want. After I get married and have children I'll probably have to get up in the middle of the night."

"By the end of the week I'm always exhausted. I need the extra sleep."

"I get up late because I stay out late."

"I owe it to myself. I hate getting up every morning at seven, but I have to to get to work on time. Weekends should be for indulging yourself."

Almost any career girl would second this last opinion. Any kind of activity, up to and including total inactivity, will do on weekends so long as it's what she wants and not what someone else tells her. Saturday and Sunday, says the consensus, ought to be entirely separate from Monday to Friday.

To start with, most girls who live on a fairly regimented nine-to-five schedule during the week prefer to let weekends take care of themselves. With the important exception of the Saturday-night date, they don't plan weekends in advance. If Barbara calls at eleven, there's a good chance Elaine will be free to have lunch with her at one.

The weather may well determine what a girl does with her days. Some say that their weekends, particularly Saturdays, depend entirely on weather. If it's nice, they usually manage to get in a long walk sometime during the day.

Walking is the second of the working girl's favorite sports. Out-of-towners and city slickers alike love it. They go to museums, to the Bowery, to Chinatown, to Central Park, to the zoo, to Greenwich Village, or just to visit a friend, and if the sun is shining they walk all the way.

"I have no way of knowing how long I'll be in the city," said a twenty-two-year-old Ohioan, "and I want to see as much of it as I can while I'm here. If I took a bus or a subway to a place I'd miss everything along the way. Most of the time I enjoy my walk more than the place I go to. You know that ad —'Getting there is half the fun'? It's true."

"Walking," declared another girl, "is the only way to get to know a city. I was born here, but I lived pretty much in one neighborhood and hardly knew that other parts of town existed. Now I'm old enough to want to see it all and to appreciate it all. I'm not tied down to my family any more and I'm not married, and there's nothing I *have* to do on weekends, so what better time to get to know the place you grew up in?"

If the neighborhood is a fairly "good" one, many young women prefer to take their walks alone. Several said they liked company when walking in Central Park, not so much because they think it's dangerous as because "there's not so much to see there so you might as well have someone to talk to."

Walking is often combined with the third of the career girl's most popular weekend pastimes: shopping. Whether it be for clothes, shoes, hats, bags, books, cheese, furniture, or simply hairpins, the shopping expedition often occupies the better part of a Saturday afternoon.

Saturdays are just about the only time a working girl has to shop. During the week she may eat a fast lunch and, if she works on or near Madison Avenue, rush to the nearest department store, but there's no time for selective shopping, only for the quick purchase of necessities. Girls who work in the Wall Street area can't even do *that* much; there are no large stores downtown. They do *all* their shopping on Saturdays.

Most girls like clothes and enjoy shopping for them, but even those who do not, feel compelled to improve their wardrobes once they start work. Many jobs require a certain standard of dress; some more so than others. Girls in the communications industries, for example, pay very close attention to appearances. Sweaters and skirts left over from college days are anathema to any self-respecting publishing, magazine, or television assistant. The few who can't or won't dress up to par are keenly aware that they look "different."

"Truthfully, I dress worse than any of the other people around," confessed a TV secretary ruefully. "I'm slightly stumped about what to wear; I just don't look right in the sort of clothes the other girls have on—tailored dresses and the like. I manage to avoid wearing the rattiest clothes I own but I know I don't meet the standard."

Conservative clothes are the rule among college girls, who generally wear "plain things—sheaths, tweed, and the like—no frills." Those who work for high-fashion women's magazines are as a group the most expensively and "dressily" dressed among young women in communications. There are, of course, exceptions. A Holyoke graduate, now twenty-five, tells of her first job as secretary in a public-relations firm. "I made up my mind," she recalls, "to knock their eyes out my first day at work. I went out and bought a shocking-pink cocktail sheath, very chic, and came to work all set for stares and whistles. As it turned out, compared to the other girls in the office I looked positively dowdy!"

The ideal in the communications world seems to be to dress nicely, but not *too* nicely. The Brooks Brothers suit who works in the next cubicle might admire the girl with the eye-catching wardrobe but he may think twice about marrying her. When a girl appears *too* interested in what she wears ("I never wear the same dress twice when I go out with a date"), a man sees dollar signs dancing before his eyes ("Sure she's attractive, but who could keep her in clothes?").

In the financial district, on the other hand, casual clothes prevail. "At college," said a research analyst, "I dressed extremely sloppily. I find here I must dress a little better, but not much. I dislike dressy clothes and hate shopping for them; when I do buy clothes I invariably wind up buying men's shirts. No, I don't look any worse than most of the others."

"I still have my college clothes," said an insurance broker's assistant. "I wear the same things over and over. In my job you don't have much contact with people outside and everyone dresses fairly informally. Sometimes we look like we're still running around campus. I wear mostly sweaters and skirts to work; plain pullovers with beads. I have four or five suits: camel hair, tweed, plaid; but I only wear a wool dress or suit if I'm meeting somebody for lunch. Hats and gloves, never.

I love to wear them on weekends, but in the office you'd just feel conspicuous."

Girls who do wear hats and gloves to the office are rare in the financial district and almost as rare uptown. They are usually one of two breeds: the fashion-magazine assistant or the Katharine Gibbs graduate. The former wears these accessories because it's the thing to do; the latter because it's been ingrained by months of repetition and training.

Katharine Gibbs girls do dress better than any group of secretaries anywhere. That's because the school considers a secretary's appearance almost as important as her skills, and gives its students, along with typing and stenography, a series of lectures on good grooming. "We feel," says a KG teacher, "that the girl should look the part. She represents the office just as a product in a package does." From the moment the prospective secretary starts school, Gibbs expects her to dress according to the standard, and, so that there may be no question in anyone's mind what the standard is, issues her a pamphlet called "Wardrobe ABC's for Gibbs Girls." Some of its high points:

> *Sheer or sleeveless blouses are covered with jackets.*
> *Shoes, usually pumps of a neat, classic style, must have heels at least one inch high.*
> *Long hair should be pinned tidily off the neck. Complicated and faddish hairdos are taboo for office wear.*
> *Appropriate: Tailored dresses, suits, trim skirts (not too tight, not too short), crisp-looking blouses, slipon sweaters (under jackets), knitted dresses and suits ("be careful of fit!"), classic, tailored hats.*
> *Inappropriate: Man-tailored shirts open at the neck, crinolines, turtle-neck or cardigan sweaters (even under jackets or jumpers), heavy jacket-type sweaters, ankle socks, loafers, ballerinas, wedgies, country shoes, hats or*

*scarves that tie under the chin, veils or narrow bands in
place of hats, dangling or pendant earrings, noisy brace-
lets, anklets.*

Gibbs girls consider the hats-and-gloves rule in particular
legitimate ground for gripes, especially since a student can
pick up a fast detention by coming to school without them.
The system is theoretically in force wherever a girl goes. (One
recent KG graduate who hated hats and only put them on as
she was entering the school premises replaced her Katharine
Gibbs book covers with NYU stickers as a precaution against
being seen hatless by a teacher on the way to school.) The
powers that be at Katharine Gibbs are used to complaints from
students and amused inquiries from outsiders, and greet them
alike with dogged determination: "We are still hanging on."

While Gibbs girls may be restricted when it comes to
shopping for weekday clothes, they and most other young
women as well go all out for dress-up dresses. Career girls as
a class are selective shoppers. That doesn't mean they hunt
around from store to store, comparing prices and looking for
bargains. They have neither the time nor, generally, the in-
clination for that. Rather than buy two or three cheap dresses
they'll buy one good one, and they know that a high price tag
doesn't necessarily mean a good dress. A Macy's senior vice
president thinks they're "the best shoppers in the world. They
are very sharp," he says. "They know the difference between
a good bargain and a bad buy. You can't fool a working girl."

Where to shop is a problem that can be bewildering; there
are so many stores and so little time. One girl buys "clothes
at Bloomingdale's, stockings and underwear at cheap places
like Klein's, and accessories and fun things at the Village
shops." Another, who works at Saks Fifth Avenue, buys all her
"important" clothes there at a 30 per cent discount, but goes

shopping for "little things" in other stores on Saturdays. One
English secretary "tried the Fifth Avenue stores and found
them fiendishly expensive"; another girl, making the same 90-
dollar salary, "wouldn't go anywhere but Fifth Avenue."

Like women everywhere, career girls prefer to shop where
they have charge accounts. Getting an account is not always
easy, especially if you're just starting your first job on a shoe-
string and have no bank references to give the store. Some
stores flatly refuse to take a chance on a beginning career girl,
and from all accounts they lose out in the end. Young
women, after they have saved some money, may open charge
accounts in stores that wouldn't take them when they first
applied, but they tend to remain loyal to the one or two
stores that did. Bloomingdale's, with its location in the heart
of career-girl territory, is one such, and several girls recalled
shopping there on a charge account when no other store
would take them. "They seem to figure young career girls are
a good bet," said one. "They were nice where other stores
were rather nasty. I got used to going there, and I still do."

The clothes a girl buys on Saturdays are seldom worn on
Sunday, unless she's a regular churchgoer or has an afternoon
cocktail party in the offing. Saturday is for dressing up;
Sunday is for lounging about in one's oldest and most comfortable Bermudas. Large late brunches are the order of the
day, followed by long sessions with the Sunday paper. Even
girls who don't buy a paper at all during the week say they
try to get through the *Times* or *Tribune* on Sundays; "There's
more than enough in the Sunday papers," said one, "to keep
me up to date the rest of the week."

Unless the weather is at its sunniest Sundays are more
likely than not to be stay-at-home days. Besides the papers,
with their jumbo crossword puzzles ("My roommate and I get

along splendidly; I love to do the Sunday puzzle and she hates it"), there are letters to be written, books to be read, Sunday-afternoon television—the only kind the career girl will admit to watching—to be seen. Bridge fans (and few girls manage to escape from college without learning to play) gather in their foursomes on Sundays.

Occasionally, if it's raining or snowing hard enough to insure that other people will stay home, girls who live in the East Fifties and Sixties go to a Sunday movie, sometimes by themselves. They wait for bad weather because: a) there won't be the usual long lines standing outside to see the latest foreign film (which is inconveniently located for most people but within walking distance if one lives where career girls live); and b) the smaller the audience, the less chance of meeting the people one least wants to meet when she's wearing soggy loafers and a trench coat thrown over her slacks. Rainy Sundays are an especial blessing to the young woman who hasn't yet made the preview-party set but whose friends and co-workers have.

If a girl doesn't mind solitude she is more likely to want Sunday to herself than any other day of the week. Conversely, the ones who hate being alone even for a minute find the day something of a trial.

"If I'm not invited to somebody else's cocktail party," said one girl, "I throw together one of my own. Nothing fancy, of course, just a little hello-why-don't-you-drop-over-and-bring-your-own-bottle kind of thing. I never quite know how it's going to turn out. Sometimes we wind up playing cards, or someone brings a guitar and we sing folk songs, or we just have a few beers and then all go out for hamburgers. I try not to have the same people all the time but it usually winds up that I mostly do."

"There are some Sundays," said another girl who frankly admitted that she is "a compulsive party giver," "when I think I'll go mad because I can't find anyone around. Days like that I'm almost tempted to go down to Roseland [a public dance hall] just to be with people having fun. I suspect certain friends of mine deliberately don't answer their phones on Sunday afternoons. I rather envy people like that who don't mind being alone for hours on end, but I'm just not made that way. I try to plan my Sundays in advance so I'll be sure to have company."

Asked if they belonged to any social clubs, political societies, or recreational groups, a majority of career girls questioned, including the party givers who were so avid for company, replied in the negative. College-educated women are apparently not, at least before marriage, "joiners," possibly because they've had enough of "belonging" in college. The farthest they usually go toward identifying with an organization is to join a professional society related to their work; one-third, say statistics, do belong to groups such as the Young Women's Investment Association or American Women in Radio and Television. Typical of the professional-society members was the girl who said she belonged to the Newspaper Guild of New York—"But no other. I am against organizations. I used to belong to my college alumnae association but I don't even do that any more."

The alumnae associations are, on the whole, having some trouble recruiting new members and holding on to old ones. While their rosters naturally show a rise from year to year as each new class graduates, the percentage of graduates joining is dropping off. Girls who do belong are often less than whole-hearted about it. "I belong to the Skidmore College Alumni Club of New York," said one girl. "It's because I can't say no. They ask me to do something and rather than argue I say I'll do it, and then I feel miserable about it. That's how I got to be treasurer for two years—a rotten job. They're the only ones who've really gotten hold of me."

Career girls don't exactly scorn "belonging"; they simply aren't interested. "I guess I'm not a belonger," they say, or, "I have just never found anything I wanted to belong to." When they *do* join something, more often than not they're apologetic about it, such as the Skidmore girl who couldn't say no or the young government worker who admitted membership in something called the Association of Former Students in Geneva in the United States, and quickly added that she "only joined because they needed funds."

In a few cases girls said they joined professional or religious organizations in order to qualify for charter flights to Europe in the summer. Young single women do not, however, make up a significant percentage of charter passengers, presumably because they only get two weeks of vacation and the charter groups normally go abroad for three weeks or more.

Europe, at any rate, is a little too expensive for the average career girl's pocketbook. If she's been there at all it was probably during the summer following graduation; partly, at least, at her parents' expense. If she hasn't been she hopes to go, maybe on her honeymoon. Meanwhile, she vacations closer to home.

Single girls do not greatly enjoy traveling alone. Roommates often go away together. Those who learned to ski at college, and there are many, usually manage to take their two weeks in the winter, when the snow covers the slopes of Vermont and New Hampshire. Skiers travel in packs, men and women together, five or six to a car, sharing gas and expenses on the way. The cost of a New England skiing trip can normally be figured at about 20 dollars a day, including travel expenses, dormitory room and board, chair-lift or rope-tow charges, equipment and entertainment. If the skier is a novice and seriously wants to learn the sport, lessons are an additional 5 dollars an hour; not surprisingly, few girls can afford the cost of an entire vacation spent learning to ski. In San Francisco and Los Angeles the skiers go to Sun Valley, Idaho.

The destinations of summer vacationers are less easy to pin down. There is a fairly general rule among them that says, "Go everywhere," and especially, "Go where the boys are." Many do have a preference for one particular area, with the Virgin Islands getting the most favorable mentions. On the East Coast, Maine, Cape Cod, and Long Island (especially East-, West-, and Southhampton) are popular, but seldom do girls stay at the same place twice.

Since their vacations are short they prefer planes, when the cost is not absolutely prohibitive, to trains and cars. "Get there as fast as you can and get the most out of it you can," seems to be the consensus.

Usually the "most" is about twenty-eight, six feet tall, and unattached. All in all, that summer paradise isn't so different from home.

What's She Really Like? | *chapter XII*

What different girls want from life—What they
hope to accomplish—How many do . . . and
don't—The suicide rate among working girls,
especially out-of-towners—The marriage rate—
Working after marriage.

"Life," said Lindsay Brower, Barnard '61, "is pretty much a
matter of goals. Everybody wants to be happy, and whether
you are depends on what you think happiness is."

The question had been, "What do you want from life?"
and the reply pretty much typified those of other unmarried
college graduates working in New York City. All of them
want "to be happy" and nearly all have different ideas of
happiness.

Young men dream of money and fame, but young women
dream of marriage. An overwhelming majority of single career
girls want, one day, to be married. In marriage some girls hope

to find "security"; others, "a home of my own." Some want children; some, social standing; a few "an escape from the constant pressure of loneliness." Many think happiness consists of having both a husband and a job; others will quit work as soon as they marry. Some girls say the simple fact of being a "Mrs." will be enough for them; they haven't, they say, thought beyond the wedding day.

Very few girls under the age of twenty-five ever give much thought to what their lives will be like if they stay single. They worry about meeting men and having a date for Saturday night. They live in the present. Marriage belongs in the future, near enough to be realistic about but far enough away to romanticize. The possibility of a permanently single life is too remote even to be contemplated.

Yet most unmarried women over thirty will remain single and at work until they retire, and among college graduates the chance of marriage after thirty is significantly lower than among non-graduates. Education directly affects the possibility of marriage, statistically. The more education a girl has, the more likely she is to work; the more she works, the longer she stays single; the longer she stays single, the less likely she is to marry.

Gloomy facts like these never yet kept an intelligent girl out of college. Most graduates would agree with the young mother who said, "If somebody told me I could either have a college education and quite possibly never get married, or not go to college and definitely get married, I'd certainly choose to go. I'd rather live alone, having had an education which enables me to be interested in a wide variety of things, than get married and maybe not know or care that there was anything else in the world but me and my family."

The value placed on higher education by college girls is

shared by young women who did not go past high school, though for different reasons. Fifty high-school graduates, surveyed some years ago in Chicago, overwhelmingly agreed that the one thing they lacked that "would make them really happy" was a college education. They saw education, however, more as an immediate aid to better jobs, higher pay, et cetera, than as a future aid to living. They were not asked, but in all probability they would not have agreed with the college-yes-marriage-maybe philosophy.

In any case, marriage is the usual answer to the question of future happiness. Career girls, however, almost always make a sharp distinction between "now" and "someday." "Do you mean," they ask, "what do I want from life *now*, or what do I want eventually?"

When the answer is "now," the responses run the whole length of the happiness spectrum from "two months in Europe" to "my boss's job." The career girl's daydreams, like anyone's, have some element of realization in them, and the closer connection they have with the immediate present, the more concrete they become. Thus, rather than a vague "Marriage will make me happy eventually," one gets a definite "I'd like a new wardrobe right now."

Business life ranks high as a center of interest among college girls (though not among non-graduates, who say the office brings more problems than pleasures), and daydreams are often connected in some way with work. Few career girls hope to get rich or famous though their jobs; they think more in terms of "accomplishment" and "satisfaction" than of fame or financial benefits. Business and money, indeed, are unconnected except insofar as one results from the other. Where a man might use an unexpected financial windfall to invest in his business or buy stocks, the average girl would travel or buy clothes. ("If I had 5000 dollars to spend just as I pleased, I'd go out and buy the clothes I really liked. A leopard coat would be first on the list. Then, instead of spending 50 dollars for a suit, I'd buy one for 250 dollars. Clothes are my weakness.")

"Accomplishment," in many cases, means promotion. "I would like by the time I get married really to have done something in my job. I would like to feel that I've exhausted the possibilities in my field [publishing] and done as much as I wanted. I would like to be able to have something to look back on that I can be proud of and maybe want to go back to someday. To be specific, I want to work my way up; to be a reader in a few months, and eventually an editor, or as close to it as I can. I think once I got to be an editor I would start looking around seriously for a husband, but till then I'm just as well off—better—unmarried. I have a long way to go toward fulfilling myself as a person before I'll be ready to cope with marriage. If I can know when I get married that I've made a success of my job, I'll have a lot more confidence about making a success of my marriage."

"When I think of what I want now," said another girl, "I naturally think in terms of my job, because that's what occupies me the most and what's most important to me at the moment. Just like in college I used to get satisfaction out of good grades, here I get it when people tell me I'm doing good work. Knowing that I'm doing well in my job is enough for me at the moment. If you ask me what I want to happen eventually, I'd have to say I hope my supervisor leaves and I get her job."

When a survey was taken in 1955 among college graduates working on their first jobs, 83 per cent said they held the type of job they'd always wanted. In 1956 the figure jumped to

85 per cent; one year later, to 86 per cent, and today it is around 91 per cent. With such a high percentage of graduates satisfied in their work, it is no wonder that so many build castles around it. People who are unhappy in the office do not dream of advancement; like the college-educated girl who somehow found herself a saleslady in a department store, they think instead of "travel—and if I didn't have enough money I'd just like to stay home for a year and rest."

Outside the business world, and excepting marriage, career girls see surprisingly few opportunities to accomplish much. They are not joiners. They derive little satisfaction from being an officer of a social or professional group. The only organized outside activity that interests more than a few is politics and, lately, the civil-rights and ban-the-bomb movements. Those girls (often former student government officers at college) who do give their time and energy to these causes say that they get tremendous satisfaction from participating in "something outside myself I can really believe in"; but, conversely, little sense of personal accomplishment because, "I can have no control over the situation—it's so much bigger than I am." "I don't think anyone has a right to feel pleased with herself for doing something she sincerely believes ought to be done," said a Sarah Lawrence graduate who had spent two days in jail for participating in a Southern sit-in. "Satisfied, yes, because she's done what she had to do, but as for congratulating herself on an 'accomplishment,' certainly not."

Those who take no active part in events are usually highly aware of what's going on, but not very many career girls worry over world problems the way they do over themselves and their work. "I keep up with the world situation in the papers and it certainly doesn't please me, but I don't worry about it. I have never given much thought to being hit by the bomb.

I'm more involved with the immediate present than with projecting into the future."

"I read a lot," said one girl. "I have to know what's going on. I once stopped reading editorials because I got scared about fallout. Then I started reading *Time* because they seemed to be so blasé about it."

Said another, "We have all the civil-defense booklets in our apartment, which is ridiculous because every time the train goes by underneath the apartment simply shakes! We're looking for a new place, but it's such a problem. If you happen to hear of any . . ."

"I think I'd be more concerned about things if I had a home and a family," mused a twenty-two-year-old. "When I get married I'll probably want a fallout shelter under the house. Now, I'm responsible only for myself and I guess I'd just run to the subway."

Responsibility for oneself looms large in the minds of career girls—larger, perhaps, than is really necessary. The transition to adulthood, runs the reasoning, will be complete only if a girl is prepared to make her own decisions and run her own life. Friends and roommates are legitimate advisers, but not parents, and going to an analyst, which was formerly regarded as rather the thing to do, is beginning to be frowned upon. Nor does religion play any significant part in the lives even of those who were brought up in the strictest traditions. While very few girls admit to actual atheism, and most immediately inform you that they believe in God, the percentage of regular churchgoers in large cities is low. Some girls are apologetic about this, but more are simply disinterested.

"I never go to church. I haven't been since '54, when I heard a sermon I didn't like. I suppose I believe in God. I think about it a lot less than I used to."

"I went to a Quaker boarding school, though I'm a Presbyterian. I rather enjoyed Quaker meetings in school, but I haven't been to church at college or since."

"I go to temple when my mother chooses to go. I quite like it. When I go out with someone religious, I go to temple with him. I'm a lot less of a rebel than I used to be, but I am not particularly concerned with God at this time."

"I once went through a religious seizure, almost. At times when I needed God He wasn't around. Now, I don't think about it."

"I don't go to synagogue regularly. In fact, not at all. At times I've gone on holy days. I was brought up in an orthodox synagogue and still have an intangible connection. I have certain guilty feelings about not observing the religion, but the intellectual break is complete."

"I have never had any deep religious experiences but I very strongly believe in God. The secular idea that science disproves God, I find shallow."

"I have had a few momentary religious experiences but never lasting ones. I do believe in God but don't go to church. I have felt sometimes that it must be nice to believe in an orthodox dogma that would make your actions clearcut and give you a whole philosophy of life. I think a lot of people *need* something greater than themselves on whom they can call."

"I don't go to church. It's about eight years since I've been. I don't know anyone who goes regularly, even those who say they are religious. The pace in a big city is too fast, life is too full. In small towns, church brings social contacts. Here, no."

Constant reminders of belief in God and the steady practice of religion, said one girl, "properly belong in families, and when I have one I've no doubt that I'll become a good Christian again. In the meantime I want to think things out for myself, without God's help or anyone else's. God won't mind waiting."

In their spare time, which usually means on dateless weekday nights, career girls do a great deal of reading. Magazines come first; almost everyone has certain favorites that she feels she *must* get through before turning to a book (which is likely to be a current best seller). The usual pattern is to subscribe to one or two magazines and buy the others on the newsstands.

Time and *Newsweek* are read most often, most thoroughly, and occasion the most violent comment ("I detest *Time*. I hate their style and I think they distort the news. I don't like their playing with other people's lives. Yes, I read it every week"). Aside from the news magazines, other favorites are *Harper's* ("if something looks interesting"), the *New Yorker* ("to be able to discuss the stories everybody else talks about; also because I like it"), *Esquire* ("it's really got some good stuff lately"), and *Vogue* ("to see what I can't afford but should be wearing"). Girls who work in government and international relations read, in addition, *The Reporter*, *The Nation*, and the *National Review* (liberals, "for laughs"; conservatives, "because it's the only news review that has intelligent ideas about politics").

In general the girls who read the most books are those who are most recently out of college. After a few years reading seems to become increasingly less important, though being "well informed" is still considered a necessity. "It gets difficult after a while for people who are alone a great deal," said a twenty-seven-year-old secretary. "In the back of my mind is always, 'I'm sitting here reading alone because I'm alone and have nothing else to do,' which spoils the enjoyment."

Young women under the age of twenty-five rarely admit to experiencing long periods of depression, and seem, if anything, to enjoy being alone. As years pass, however, loneliness becomes something of a problem and girls become increasingly aware that they have time on their hands that they must fill by themselves. "When I haven't anything else to do," said a twenty-nine-year-old editor, "I take myself to a show. Usually I like the depressing ones—Tennessee Williams—the best. The more depressing it is, the better I like it. It's cathartic, I guess."

Thoughts of suicide, which nearly everyone entertains at some time or other, are often in her mind, the editor added, but, she said, she had no fear that matters would ever come to such a crisis. "It would be cowardly not to give myself a chance in life. By the time I'm fifty I want to know that I've at least tried."

No one can determine the actual number of suicides, or attempts at suicide, in any one year among unmarried career girls. For one thing, details of suicides are unavailable for research; for another, probably five successful suicides go unrecorded to every one that gets into the papers—and the number of unrecorded attempts is much larger. Even if the exact number were known it would tell little, unless the reasons could also be known, and this is impossible.

There is an organization in New York City called "Save-A-Life" that exists solely for the purpose of deterring would-be suicides. From their files, which are necessarily limited to persons working in New York, certain cautious conclusions may be drawn. First: loneliness is the main problem among girls who contemplate suicide. Second: three times as many men as women commit suicide, but women try more often. Third: of the women, a majority are out-of-towners, usually living alone in small apartments or hotels. Fourth: the people who request assistance from Save-A-Life are normally those who have had some crisis in their lives, often preceded by a culmination of depressing experiences, rather than the chronically ill.

Some idea of the type of girl who becomes suicidal may be gained by giving a few of the organization's case histories, which are factual rather than analytic. These must of necessity be set forth in capsule form, as Save-A-Life is understandably reluctant to discuss its cases beyond their bare essentials.

1.) R.C., aged 27. Californian; M.A. degree from U.C.L.A. Parents divorced. Disliked her mother and was disliked by her in return. Was making $125 a week in advertising when she lost her job after a series of affairs with men in the office. Had a breakdown but recovered and went back to work. Unhappy in her new job; voluntarily institutionalized herself for five weeks. Mother traveled to New York to see her; made matters worse by insisting R.C. had brought it on herself. Unsuccessful suicide attempt, followed by first contact with Save-A-Life. Mother later relented and offered to pay for further psychiatric care.

2.) J.H., age 29. Nice-looking, homespun type. Living in New Jersey with mother. Three married sisters. Making $90 a week as a private secretary in New York. Starting to feel she'd given up a lot for mother. Sisters wanted mother to live with them but mother had clamped on to J.H. Never dated men, only went out with other girls. Hated it. No prospects in town for marriage; at work, all the men were married. Felt in a rut. Other than church choir, not much in her life. Contemplated suicide but was put in touch with Save-A-Life and never attempted it.

3.) H.B.C., age 23. A Midwesterner, B.A. Ohio State. Wanted to be a commercial artist but couldn't get a job. Went to work in a department store meanwhile. Living in a residence house. Pressed for money and could not pay hotel bill. She explained the situation to the hotel manager and thought he said he'd wait for payment, but apparently misunderstood him. Went home one winter night and found her room padlocked. Rushed up to Save-A-Life hatless and coatless and threatened suicide. Save-A-Life called the hotel and talked to the manager, telling him it might have caused a terrible catastrophe. Manager relented immediately. "Tell her to come right down here and we'll take care of it. Anything she wants."

Young men sometimes appear in the offices of Save-A-Life to say that they are dating girls whose fathers or mothers committed suicide, and to inquire if this runs in families. The organization does its best to reassure them that it does not. Actually, any girl who has a boy friend interested enough in her to make such an inquiry is a giant step ahead of those who do not, for she at least does not have to cope with the problem of loneliness.

Marriage, it has been said time and again, is not a panacea. It should perhaps be added that the *idea* of marriage, or even just of having a steady boy friend, is. "I am bothered by sex, and so is every other unmarried woman," declared a twenty-eight-year-old secretary, adding, "I don't know that I would even have to get married to be less lonely—just to feel that there was somebody around I *might* marry someday."

But thousands of other young women want "somebody around" too. The competition is intense, though things are not really as bad as one cynical forty-three-year-old bachelor believes. "Any man who goes to the expense of keeping a woman nowadays," he said, "is either very dumb or very unattractive to women. There are so many girls around that a bachelor doesn't have to look further than his own apartment building to find one. No wonder girls complain about how hard it is to find a good husband. The men can afford to take their time. Morals have changed completely since I was a young man. Now so many girls are ready to hop into bed with a man that the 'good' girls don't stand a chance."

Luckily for the "good" girls, there are still plenty of men who, when they finally start looking for a wife, look in their direction. Of a recent Mount Holyoke class, 93 per cent of the graduates were married within five years after graduation, and Holyoke has never been noted for widespread immorality.

Almost all career girls who do marry before they're thirty continue working, at least until children come. For many, this year or two is one of the happiest times of their lives—"All the delights of holding down an interesting job," said one, "and none of the pressures from having half your mind set on sizing up the men around."

After the family is begun there comes a period of perhaps ten years, during which time the young mother stays at home with the children. When the youngest enters kindergarten, however, she is quite likely—especially if she's a college graduate—to go back to work.

There are three major groups of "returners," as the employment agencies call them. One consists of the young mothers who must bring in added income to support a growing family until their husbands' firms decide they're ready for promotion. Another group is made up of the women at the opposite age extreme, usually widows who are having a hard

time living on their husbands' reduced social-security payments. These older women, sixty and up, normally hold
temporary or part-time jobs to supplement their incomes.

In between these two financially motivated groups comes
the third, whose reasons for returning to work are somewhat
more complex. They are often college graduates, and the
writer of the following letter is typical.

> *"Now that my youngest child is in school, I know that
> I will have to do something or I will turn into one of
> those selfish, smothering mothers that cannot let go
> and that try to live vicariously through their children.
> I am only thirty-four and why should I live as a parasite
> on my hard-working husband?"*

Her husband is at work. Her children are old enough to
have their own interests and friends. She feels trapped, use-
less, bored, frustrated, lonely. More than anything, she needs
to be needed, and a full- or part-time job is the ideal solution
to her problem.

College-educated married women with school-age children
are much more likely to return to work than those who did
not go to college, assuming that there is no financial need in
either case. Among the college-educated it is becoming something of a social stigma to "sit home alone doing nothing," in
direct contrast to non-college women, who tend to regard
families in which the wife works as somewhat lower on the
social scale than themselves. According to U. S. Labor Department statistics the college woman today can look forward
to twenty-five years of working experience during her lifetime, and only seven of those years come before marriage.
The figures speak for themselves.

Onward and Upward | *chapter XIII*

The career girl: her place in business—What
she can aspire to—Discrimination against women
in different industries—The determined woman
—The mannish woman—The girl who takes ad-
vantage of her sex—What men say about career
girls: her boy friends, her co-workers.

On the thirty-sixth floor of a Madison Avenue office building
there is a long corridor carpeted entirely in thick green wool.
About a dozen offices line the hall at twenty-foot intervals;
each door bears, in heavy greenish-gold lettering, the name of
a man.

Just beyond the last door the corridor turns sharp right into
a wide L, and in the one enormous room formed by the
base of the letter sits an alert figure wearing a trim blue suit,
light sweater, and single strand of pearls.

Her name is Alice Costello, and at the age of forty-six she

is vice president and general manager in charge of promotion at one of the largest advertising agencies in the nation. Earning a salary of 22,000 dollars a year, she is about as close to the top of her field as any woman could hope to be.

No one in the firm knew that, as of the spring of 1964, Miss Costello was planning to leave. None of the twelve men who worked directly under her suspected that one of them would very shortly be taking over her job. But their boss knew it all along, right from the day she moved into the L-shaped office at the end of the corridor.

"When I got this job they told me, 'Alice, we hope you'll take a long-range view of things. Don't hesitate to plan fifteen years ahead. The job is yours as long as you want it.' In other words, 'Here you are and here you'll stay.'

"Well, I've stayed five years. I know all there is to know about the job. There's no challenge any more. But there's no sense sitting around, hoping for a promotion. Any one of the messenger boys downstairs has a better chance of becoming president of this firm than I do."

That's why she will shortly leave the company.

"Women in business can go just so far and not a step farther. I seem to have gone about as far as I can go."

According to time-honored business tradition, Alice Costello actually went a lot farther than she should have. For most women, promotion ends where the supervision of men begins.

"It's not that we have anything against women as women," explained the personnel manager of Miss Costello's firm, "but so many of our workers are men, and they seem to prefer working under other men."

What makes it even harder for the hopeful career girl is that women do too. Employers are not quite sure why this should be ("Maybe because they think they can get away with more," said one; "Probably because our society is accustomed to men giving orders and women taking them," said another), but more often than not an all-girl department will have a male supervisor. It has been said that the quickest way for a man to get ahead in business is to join a firm where most of the employees are women.

Discrimination against women in business is nothing new. In fact, as any girl who has ever worked anywhere knows, men expect it and women accept it. Most women simply couldn't care less, because they haven't the vaguest intention of making the office a permanent fixture in their lives. They know perfectly well that they won't ever get to the point where some man might want their job.

Among college girls, who are more likely to hold administrative and executive positions eventually, this "it's-got-nothing-to-do-with-me-so-why-fight-it?" attitude is widespread. A government survey of single college women in the class of 1957, made soon after graduation, asked nearly 100,000 girls their plans for future employment. The replies:

Plan to have a career	19%
Plan to work indefinitely but have no interest in a career	10%
Plan to work only as necessary for economic reasons	4%
Plan to stop work when I have children	33%
Plan to work a short while after marriage	25%
Plan to quit when married	9%

Suppose that these responses had come from men, not women. If 67 per cent of American men quit work when they became husbands or fathers, our birth rate might soar but it wouldn't be long before all those new babies were living in caves. As things now stand, and as they always will unless someone invents a substitute for mothers, the burden of keeping our economy going falls first and foremost on the man.

This being so, it is hardly astonishing that men prefer to hire qualified men for executive jobs over equally and sometimes better qualified women. Long-established customs have a way of dying hard, and most women, as the survey shows, make it all very simple by not wanting the jobs anyway.

For the 19 per cent of college graduates who "definitely plan to have a career," life will not always be easy. (Nineteen per cent, incidentally, is probably far too high a figure. Many of the girls who said they wanted a career may not have been thinking in terms of a permanent job. Alice King, head of New York's Alumnae Advisory Center, makes a distinction. "It's my feeling that the word 'career' doesn't mean what it did ten years ago. It's a temporary frame of mind now, between college and marriage. They're dedicated to a *life* career, not a job career.")

Still, supposing that 19 per cent of all graduates in a given year, or about 30,000 women, really intend to find a job and stay with it till retirement age, how far up the business ladder can they expect to climb?

It depends partly on the profession they pick. Apart from traditional women's fields such as education and social work, in which women hold at least as many top jobs as men, girls can expect to encounter some degree of resistance in almost any field. The communications industries, which employ a high percentage of persons of "liberal" bent, are a good bet, although several of our largest news and family magazines are notoriously male-dominated. Women's magazines discriminate, as might be expected, in a girl's favor. Newspapers are almost sure to have a solidly male staff of editors, always excepting their women's page. In publishing women can become editors in the areas of children's books, cookbooks, school textbooks, and the like, but fiction, documentaries, science, biographies, and books of "general interest" are more often edited by men. Advertising, as Alice Costello said, lets a girl get just so far and no farther. Some of the industry's top copywriters are women; where women's products such as hosiery, jewelry, clothing are concerned, almost invariably so. But few women reach the executive level and the number of female heads of agencies is infinitesimal. Women fare little better in television and radio. They do become announcers, newswriters, and interviewers (also weather girls), but seldom are they in a position to dictate the station's policies.

Non-profit organizations and foundations do employ women on high levels, perhaps because the people they deal with (colleges, museums, welfare organizations) also have many female administrators. The Ford Foundation and the Rockefeller Foundation; the American Field Service and the Experiment in International Living, to name some of the largest, employ many highly competent women executives.

Banking, insurance, and general finance have always been male preserves, and they are still poison to the average woman. Lately, though, there have been some signs of progress. Eastern women's colleges are beginning to turn out more and more mathematics and economics majors who are sincerely determined upon careers in their fields, and these girls are becoming research analysts, security analysts, and even investment counselors to some of Wall Street's largest firms. In New York most of them belong to the fifty-member

Young Women's Investment Association; one of whose members is an officer in a bank, the first woman executive in the bank's hundred-and-nine-year history. While these girls are not reaching for the moon ("We don't expect to become partners"), they do consider themselves pioneers in a field that, they say, will open up significantly to women in years to come. Most of them regard their jobs as natural results of a rapidly changing economy. "I think," said one, "that bankers and brokers suddenly realized that women numbered significantly among their clients." For their part, men are starting to agree with the stockbroker who said, with reluctant admiration, that "Any woman who has the guts to want to stay in this bloody business deserves to go as far as a man."

Law, like finance, is not and probably never will be a woman's field. There are only seven thousand women lawyers in America and the majority of them never see the inside of a courtroom. Routine divorces, wills, and estates, and legal specialties such as theatrical law, occupy many women lawyers; trusts, taxes, and corporation law, which are the profession's most important and remunerative fields, are left, on the whole, to men. Several large Wall Street firms absolutely will not employ women, and those that do usually tuck them away in back offices where they are safe from the eyes of clients. Not surprisingly women lawyers in New York City often strike out on their own, and some have done extremely well in general practice for themselves. Several such women report that the bulk of their clients are male; women, apparently, prefer to entrust their legal problems to men.

Retailing is a field in which qualified women can go far. If not many do, it is only because most are more interested in the buying and selling aspects than in the management, or business side. Being a buyer for a large department store,

with all that it involves in the way of fashion shows, lunch-
eons, and semi-annual trips to Paris, is a dream job for a
woman, and few would give it up to sit all day in an office, no
matter how high-sounding the title on the door. You can't
blame them either, because a girl doesn't become a buyer
without first serving a long, hard apprenticeship in a series
of low-paying, sometimes exhausting jobs.

Personnel work attracts many women and there is no limit
to how far they can go. If a girl is interested in "working with
people," but has neither the patience nor the desire to teach
nor the dedication needed to be a social or welfare worker,
this may be just the field for her. Many employers claim
that women make better personnel managers than men
("Maybe it's women's instinct," said one, "that makes them
see the juice where a man would see a lemon"). In New
York City several former woman personnel managers have
gone on to found their own employment agencies, and on a
list of ten of the city's top agencies eight are headed by
women. Personnel work is not usually considered "glamorous," but, like teaching and medicine, it can be among the
most satisfying of professions.

In almost any field involving the sale of products, be it
marketing, retailing, advertising, or what have you, there are
some jobs women will never get, simply because they require
"entertainment activities" that might be a source of embar-
rassment to a girl. Apart from the "Bill-Brown's-in-town;-
show-him-the-city-and-find-him-a-girl" episodes, there are con-
ventions to be attended every year at which a woman rep-
resentative would put a large crimp in the style of the male
delegates, with resulting ill will toward the company that had
the lack of foresight and tact to send her.

Career women, unless they head their own firms, must be

prepared to face one more obstacle that, though not as final as a flat refusal to give the girl the job, can be even more depressing. This is the attitude, persistent even among the most enlightened employers, that a woman doing a "man's job" should nevertheless be paid a "woman's salary."

Although nearly half the states in the union have now adopted "equal-pay-for-equal-work" resolutions, and though bills proposing that the principle be made federal law are always up before Congress, women, except those in government and civil-service jobs, usually earn less than men doing identical work. Although one study of the situation concludes that "the salary differentials between men and women get less as the job becomes more skilled," pay gaps are still commonplace on the executive and administrative levels. One problem for the people who would outlaw this kind of discrimination is that women themselves are often so grateful simply to *have* the executive jobs that they don't want to do anything to upset the apple cart—so they accept their smaller paychecks in silence. When the difference is *too* great, they may register some feeble protest, but seldom do they demand more money.

"I make 5000 dollars a year," said the twenty-six-year-old art editor of a quality magazine. "The men editors in the other departments all make 40 to 50 dollars a week more than I. That means they get a three-week vacation—people who make over 7500 dollars a year all get three weeks. If you make under that you get just two weeks. But even if I don't make what those boys do, I do as much work as they. So I am going to ask for another week's vacation."

This girl knows perfectly well that if she doesn't want the job at the salary the publisher's willing to pay her, another girl does. As far back as 1877 the Girl's Friendly Society of Boston had this point put to it in an address improbably titled "Real and Fancied Hardships of Working Girls." "As surely as water will flow downhill," declared the speaker of the day, "so will the rate of wages fall as low as the cheapest laborers will accept. . . ." The society's grandmothers could have told them the same thing. In 1831 the average weekly earnings for women in New England's cotton factories ranged from 2.20 to 2.60; for men, from 4.50 to 7.00.

Agitation for equal pay always meets resistance, and can sometimes have disastrous effects, especially on low-salaried "blue-collar" jobs. On the West Coast there was a recent case of a plant that stopped hiring women altogether after state law decreed that their pay be made equal with men, on the grounds that men were more efficient and therefore more economical. After most of the women in the factory had been thrown out of work, they asked to be taken back—and the plant did take them back, at their original salaries.

On the whole, women seem to resent job discrimination by sex more than unequal pay for equal work, probably because the latter at least allows them to do the work they want to do while the former denies them even that much.

Career girls have their own term for sex discrimination. They call it "the glass wall," because it's invisible until you try to walk through it.

Some, resigned to the inevitable, are satisfied to stop where the wall begins. Others try to fight their way through with the very weapon that kept them out in the first place. Their battle begins after five, when the filing cabinets close and the liquor closet opens.

"I'd do anything—and I mean anything—to get ahead."

Victoria A., thirty-three and blond, is the head auditor in her firm of chartered accountants; the first in the company's history to wear skirts. She sports a year-round tan from "frequent business trips down South." So does her boss.

"I'm not in love with him or anything. My career is what's important. I seem to be doing pretty well so far, wouldn't you say?"

"The men around here detest her," confided a woman typist, "and I guess you really can't blame them. They can't compete, so they take it out another way: they give her the barest minimum of co-operation. Work is never finished on time. Things are always getting fouled up.

"The boss doesn't notice it now, but he's sure to eventually, and that'll be the end of her."

If the typist's prediction is correct, the sunburned Miss A. is in for a rude shock. Maybe she won't be so impatient about getting ahead in her next job.

Men resent a woman who takes advantage of her sex but laugh at one who belittles it. You can spot her in almost any crowd: the female executive who walks, talks, thinks, drinks, acts, and looks like a man.

"I thought I'd seen everything till she walked in here," said a young bank guard, nodding at a fortyish woman sitting bolt upright in a space reserved for "bank officers only." "Hardly a day goes by when she doesn't say something to remind me of my father."

"She's a tough one, all right," agreed a teller. "You don't see many like her any more—the beat-the-boys-at-their-own-game type. She's very efficient, but in my book her appearance and manner are dead against her."

As the man said, this breed of cat is rapidly disappearing. It flowered in the days of suffragism, died out during the depression, and reappeared in war years when women took over many jobs hitherto reserved for the male. During the early forties no one cared what she looked like as long as her work was good. The nation needed her and nothing else mattered. As President Roosevelt said, "Don't talk to me about [the lack of] manpower any more, because the manpower question has been solved by womanpower."

At the war's end women stayed in industry—and men came back. Any employer who wanted to hire a man, could. He didn't have to take an imitation when the real thing was available. When he did hire a woman he expected her to look like one. Today's career girl acts a feminine part.

Only not too feminine. The shy, sweet, helpless type may get top marks with the boys in the office, but she seldom makes the grade at promotion time. Efficiency and output—that's "output," not "putout"—is the mark of the successful career girl.

A few men there are, and always will be, who regard efficiency in a woman with the benevolence of a Borgia. They blame the working girl for everything from unemployment to radioactivity.

"It is treason to our nation to employ women!" thunders the National Men's Legion, which is headquartered in New York. "Abolish all female labor! Repeal the nineteenth amendment! Stop college education for women!"

Fortunately for the country's economy, this vociferous group is in a tiny minority. Most men have no objection to businesswomen, just so long as they confine their work to office hours.

"I took out a girl I met at a party, who worked for a big Broadway producer," recalled a young salesman. "She spent the whole time talking about her boss. She seemed to think there was nobody like him in the world. She was telling me things like what cigarette he smokes, where he goes for lunch—things like that. What do I care where he goes for lunch?

"Imagine getting married to a girl like that. You wouldn't know whether you were kissing your wife or David Merrick."

It is a truth of our society that a man can bring his work into the home and a woman, except in very special cases, cannot.

"I divorced my first wife," said a TV production assistant who has since remarried. "She used to work for a publisher. When paperback books came in she was given a pretty responsible job. She'd come home and talk, talk, talk about this and that—how the firm was expanding, how they relied on her for everything, how prospects were so great and she'd probably be an editor pretty soon.

"If she'd kept quiet about the office everything would have been fine, but it got worse and worse. After a while I got to feeling I couldn't compete with her any more."

Financially independent women come in for their share of male resentment too, not so much because of the money they earn as because of the money they insist upon spending.

"I'm not the richest guy in the world," said a commercial artist. "Half the girls I date probably make more than I do. But that doesn't give them the right to make a big scene about splitting a check in a restaurant, with the waiter and everybody watching.

"Or on a subway they'll whip out a token and go through while I'm getting change. I know they can afford it. They're not proving anything to me. But if they think I appreciate it they couldn't be more wrong."

The career girl's male co-workers, like her boy friends, don't object to what she's doing; only to what it's doing to her.

" 'Where is chivalry?' they all want to know," commented

an architect. "Well, I can tell you where it is, it's nowhere. And I can tell you why, too. Girls just don't *let* you do anything for them any more. When I meet a girl from my office in the elevator, do you think she'll even let me call out the floor? No. She's got to do everything herself. Then when we get to the floor and I try to stand aside to let her pass she gives me an elbow in the ribs and rushes out as if she's afraid I'll change my mind and try to get out ahead of her. Well, someday I damn well will."

A smart career girl can avoid these pitfalls with the greatest of ease. All she need remember is that a man wants to feel like a man.

In a want ad that has since become a classic, a prospective employer summed it all up. He was looking for an "experienced, personable career women—" someone who, as he put it, "looks like a girl, acts like a lady, thinks like a man, and works like a horse."

A